# Sugar Flowers

*for*
## cake decorating

# Sugar Flowers
## *for*
## cake decorating

NH
NEW
HOLLAND

First published in 2008 by New Holland Publishers (UK) Ltd
London • Cape Town • Sydney • Auckland

Garfield House
86–88 Edgware Road
London W2 2EA
United Kingdom
www.newhollandpublishers.com

80 McKenzie Street
Cape Town 8001
South Africa

Unit 1, 66 Gibbes Street
Chatswood
NSW 2067
Australia

218 Lake Road
Northcote
Auckland
New Zealand

ISBN 978 1 84773 122 7

Senior Editor  Corinne Masciocchi
Designer  Zoe Mellors
Photographer  Sue Atkinson
Production  Hazel Kirkman
Editorial Direction  Rosemary Wilkinson

1 3 5 7 9 10 8 6 4 2

Reproduction by Colour Scan Overseas, Singapore
Printed and bound by Craft Print International, Singapore

**For Kit**

I would like to thank all the folks who have helped me with the production of this book.
To Sue Atkinson for creating such beautiful photographs and being so great to work with!
To Corinne, my editor, for being so very patient with me during the writing of this book and
suffering tales of the wasps' nest, Siamese cats and my house move, too. A huge thank you to
all my friends who have helped me along the way in too many ways to mention: to Heather
Graham and her Siamese cat Charlie for sparking the inspiration for the cake on pages 112–3;
Kristofer Kerrigan-Graham for casting an artistic eye over many of the cakes, in particular the
Fleur-de-Lys cake (132–3); Lizzi and Kiki for so many cat hairs! To Allan Erhorn for cutting
many of the odd shaped dummy cakes and supplying several veiners used in this book;
Sathya for accommodation, support and constructive comments too!; Christine Giles for
supplying the ribbon on pages 120–1; Beverley Dutton at Squires Kitchen for the never ending
pots of vine green petal dust; Sandra David, Alex Julian and Ann Parker for last-minute
computer loans. To Alice Christie, Tombi Peck and Tony Warren for keeping me insane, and
always being there for me... and also to John Quoi Hoi for the beautiful green butterflies.
And finally to Avril and Allen Dunn – the greatest parents any sugarcrafter could wish for.

# Contents

# Introduction

*I am regularly asked to teach sugar flowers that are not only suitable for cakes, but interesting and unusual too. It is often a daunting task trying to figure out which way to jump with this request as personal taste always gets in the way, and something that interests me might not necessarily interest others.*

I have been making flowers for over 20 years and have become well accustomed to the constant demand for sugar roses on cakes. That is fine for both the customer and recipient but in order to keep my interest alive in what started out as a hobby and a passion, I like to use more unusual flowers and foliage to enhance my displays and create my own personal style, too, along the way.

Flower making is a very time consuming practice and often you will find that the long hours spent making sugar flowers compared with the realistic amount you could charge for your work never really add up, so my advice is to try and enjoy the process of creating cakes and flowers as much as possible by varying the floral content.

There have been many trends and fashions that have come and gone – in fairly recent times there has been much interest in chocolate wedding cakes and even cupcakes too! No accounting for taste – I am personally still a huge fan of the majestic rich fruitcakes as these are firmer to decorate, allowing one to achieve a smoother finish in the final sugar coating and can be worked on for longer periods of time. However, through all of these passing trends flowers remain a constant form of inspiration in the design of wedding and celebration cakes.

In this book I have tried to create flowers, foliage and cake designs that will appeal to both the novice and experienced cake decorator. The designs are purely my take on how flowers can be used on cakes and hopefully you will be able to combine and create the flowers featured in this book to produce your own individual style.

# Flower-making equipment

*Sugarflowers can be made with very little equipment — some items such as a non-stick board and rolling pin are essential, however, over a period of time you will find the other items listed below an enormous help to improve and speed up the flower-making process.*

## Non-stick board and rolling pin

These are both essential additions to the flower-maker's workbox. Avoid white boards as they strain the eyes too much. Some boards can be very shiny, making it difficult to frill the petals against it. If this is the case, simply roughen up the surface using some fine glass paper prior to use or you could turn the board over and use the back which is often less shiny. I always use a thin layer of white vegetable fat rubbed into the surface of the board, removing most of the excess with dry kitchen paper – this stops the paste sticking to the board and also makes you check each time to see if it is clean from food colour.

## Scissors

These are essential. Large florists' scissors are great for cutting wires, stamens, thread and even large petals. Finer embroidery and curved scissors are very useful for cutting fine petals, thread and ribbons, too.

## Pliers and wire cutters

Small, fine-nose pliers are another essential. Good quality pliers from electrical supply shops are best – they are expensive but well worth the investment. Electrical wire cutters are useful, too, for cutting heavier wires.

## Foam pads

These are great to place petals and leaves on while you soften the edges – especially if you have hot hands that tend to dissolve the petals as you are working them. Prior to buying this product check that it has a good surface as some have rough, open textured surfaces that will both tear the edges of your petals or leave marks on them. I either prefer the large blue pad called a Billy's Block or the yellow Celpad.

## Wires and floristry tape

Wires are available in many colours – I buy mostly white paper-covered wires, preferring to colour or tape over as I work. The quality varies between brands. The most consistent in quality are the Japanese Sunrise Wires. These are available from 35-gauge (very fine but rare) to 18-gauge (the thickest size available). Floristry tape is used in the construction of stems and bouquets. It contains a glue that is released when the tape is stretched. I am quite fussy about which tape I buy. I use mainly nile green tape from the Lion Brand tape company. White, beige, brown, twig, yellow, pink and dark red can be useful too. Some of the brands of tape are very harsh to work with – they have a strong crayon-type smell to them and should be avoided at all costs as they will hurt your fingers as you work with them.

## Tape shredder

Some cake decorators hate this gadget. I find that if it is used properly it saves a lot of time and energy. The tool contains three razor blades to cut floristry tape into quarter widths. I have a couple of tape shredders and have removed two blades from one of them so that it cuts the tape into half widths. It is often best to use a tiny amount of cold cream rubbed onto the blades with a cotton bud and also a little onto the lid that presses against the blades – this will help the tape run smoothly against the blades as it can often stick due to an excess of glue left behind from the tape. It is also wise to remove any excess build up of glue from the blades, using fine-nose pliers and also to replace the blades regularly. Handle with care at all times.

## Paintbrushes

Good quality, synthetic brushes or synthetic-blend brushes from art shops are best. I use mainly short, flat, not too soft bristle brushes for applying layers of food colour dusts to flowers and leaves. It is best to keep brushes for certain colours so you don't have to wash them after each use. I use finer sable or synthetic-blend brushes for painting fine lines or detail spots onto petals.

## Flower cutters

When I first started cake decorating over 20 years ago, there was a fairly limited selection of flower cutters available from cake decorating shops. Now there is an enormous quantity of both metal and plastic cutters to choose from. Flowers may be made using templates or freestyle techniques, however, the use of cutters creates speed and consistent accuracy of shape. I use mostly metal cutters as I can alter the shape of these if required to suit other flowers than the one it was intended to make. Many of the more interesting leaf shapes with serrated edges and intricate designs are available in plastic.

### Leaf and petal veiners

These are made from food-grade silicone rubber. They are very useful for creating natural petal and leaf texturing to sugarwork. The moulds are made using mostly real plant material to give the finished sugar flower a realistic finish. Like the flower cutters, there is a huge selection of commercial veiners to choose from.

### Stamens

There is a huge selection of commercial stamens available from cake decorating shops. I use mainly fine white and seed-head stamens, which I can then colour with powder colours.

### Thread

Fine cotton thread is best for stamens. I use lace-making Brock 120 white thread, although some thicker threads may also be useful for larger flowers. An emery board is great for fluffing up the tips of the thread to form anthers.

### Posy picks

These are made from food-grade plastic and come in various sizes. They are used to hold the handle of a spray or bouquet of flowers into the cake. The food-grade plastic protects the cake of contamination from the wires and floristry tape used in the construction of the floral spray. Never push wires directly into a cake.

### Glue

Non-toxic glue sticks can be bought from stationery or art shops and are great for fixing ribbon to the board edge. Always make sure that the glue does not come into direct contact with the cake. I use a hi-tack non-toxic craft glue to attach stamens to the ends of wires. I feel that no harm is being done sticking inedible items together with another inedible item. However, the glue should not come into direct contact with the sugar petals as it will dissolve them.

### Florists' staysoft

This is basically the soft modelling material that I used to play with as a child. It can be bought in blocks of various colours from florists' suppliers, art shops and some cake decorating shops, too. This medium should be placed into a vase or onto a thin board to protect the cake surface. As the name implies, the medium stays fairly firm but soft which is great for arranging sugar flowers into as the flowers can be removed and rearranged if needed.

### Modelling tools

*Metal ball tools (Cc) (Celcakes)*
I use mostly metal ball tools to work the edges of petals and leaves. These are heavier than plastic tools, which means that less effort is needed to soften the paste. I mostly work the tool using a rubbing or rolling action against the paste, positioning the tool half on the petal/leaf edge and half on my hand or foam pad that the petal is resting against. Metal ball tools can also be used to 'cup' or hollow out petals to form interesting shapes.

*Dresden/veining tool (J) (PME)*
The fine end of this tool is great for adding central veins to petals or leaves and the broader end can be used for working the edges of a leaf to give a serrated effect or a 'double frilled' effect on the edges of petals. Simply press the tool against the paste repeatedly to create a tight frilled effect or pull the tool against the paste on a non-stick board to create serrations. The fine end of the tool can also be used to cut into the edge of leaves and to cut and flick finer serrated-edge leaves. I use a black tool by Jem for finer, smaller leaves and flowers, and the larger yellow PME tool for larger flowers.

*Plain-edge cutting wheel (PME) and sharp scalpel*
The plain-edge cutting wheel is rather like a double-sided small pizza wheel. It is great for cutting out quick petals and leaves and also for adding division lines to buds. A sharp scalpel is also essential for marking veins, adding texture and cutting out petal shapes, too.

*Ceramic tools (HP – Holly Products)*
I use a smooth ceramic tool for curling the edges of petals and hollowing out throats of small flowers as well as using it as a mini rolling pin. The silk veining tool is wonderful for creating delicate veins and frills to petal edges

*Celsticks (Cc – Celcakes)*
There are four sizes of these small rolling pin-type tools. As well as being great for rolling out small petals and leaves to create thick ridges, the pointed end of the tool is ideal for opening up the centre of 'hat'-type flowers, such as jasmine, tweedia and paphia The rounded end can be used in the same way as a ball tool to soften edges and hollow out petals.

*Kitchen paper rings*
These basic formers are great for drying petals that require a cupped shape. The open loops allow the flowerpaste to breathe so that it dries faster than if placed into a plastic or other type of former. To make, cut strips of kitchen paper and twist back onto themselves and then tie into a loop. Larger formers can be made by cutting the kitchen paper sheet in half diagonally and then twisting – these are useful for much larger petals that require support while drying.

# Techniques

*There are many different techniques that can be used*

*to create petals and leaves – below are some*

*of the methods that I use most often.*

## FLOWER-MAKING TECHNIQUES

### Wiring petals and leaves

This is my favourite method of constructing flowers. It gives the flower much more movement and also extra strength, resulting in fewer breakages.

**1** Knead a piece of flowerpaste and roughly form it into the shape of the petal or leaf you are making. Press it down against a non-stick board to flatten it slightly. Use a celstick or rolling pin to roll the paste, leaving a ridge for the wire. Try to create a tapered ridge, angling the pin slightly so that the ridge is thicker at the base of the petal or leaf. The thickness and length of the ridge will depend on the size of the petal/leaf you are making. There are also boards available commercially which have grooves in them that create a similar ridged effect when the paste is rolled over them. These can be great for smaller petals and leaves but I find they produce too fine a ridge for many of the larger flowers that I make.

**2** Cut out the petal or leaf shape using a cutter, scalpel or plain-edge cutting wheel, leaving the ridge to run down the centre. If you are using a cutter, lift up the shape and place it onto a very light dusting of cornflour and then press firmly with the cutter and scrub it slightly against the paste and the board so that the shape remains slightly stuck in the cutter. This will enable you to quickly rub the edge of the cutter to create a cleaner cut edge, removing any fuzzy bits!

**3** Moisten the wire very slightly – too much moistness will result in the paper coming off the wire and also slow down the drying process of the petal on the wire. Hold the ridge firmly between your finger and thumb, and hold the wire in the other hand very close to the end of the wire that is being inserted into the shape. Push the wire in gradually so that it supports a third to half the length. Continue forming the shape following the instructions for each individual flower or leaf in the book.

### Working with flowerpaste

The paste should be well kneaded before you start to roll out or model it into a flower shape, otherwise it has a tendency to dry out and crack around the edges. This is an air-drying paste so when you are not using it make sure it is well wrapped in a plastic bag. If you have cut out lots of petals cover them over with a plastic bag.

### Egg white

You will need fresh egg white to stick petals together and to sometimes alter the consistency of flowerpaste if it is too dry. Many cake decorators avoid the use of fresh egg white because of the risk of salmonella. I continue to use Lion Brand eggs and always work with a fresh egg white each time I make flowers. There are commercially available edible glues which can be used instead of egg white – but I find that these tend to dissolve the sugar slightly before allowing it to dry resulting in weak petals.

### White vegetable fat

I use this to grease the non-stick board and then wipe it off with dry kitchen paper. This not only conditions the board, helping prevent the flowerpaste sticking in places to it, but also removes excess food colour that might have been left from the previous flower-making session. You can also add a tiny amount of white fat to the paste if it is very sticky – however, you must not add too much as it will make the paste short and slow down the drying process too much. You must also be careful not to leave too much fat on the board as greasy patches will show up on the petals when you start to apply the dry dusting colours.

### Cornflour bag

An essential if you have hot hands like mine! Cornflour is a lifesaver when the flowerpaste is sticky. Strangely, it is best to make a cornflour bag using disposable nappy liners! Fold a couple of layers of nappy liners together and add a good tablespoon of cornflour on top. Tie together into a bag using ribbon or an elastic band. This bag is then used to lightly dust the paste prior to rolling it out and also on petals and leaves before they are placed into a veiner.

### Colouring

Colouring is a very important part of both flowermaking and cake decorating. Colours and colour combinations are a very personal thing – I prefer slightly brighter and more unusual colour combinations than just sugar almond pink and blue! Below are listed the forms of colour that are available to the cake decorator. If you are attaching an edible decoration directly onto a cake it is important check that the colours you are using are completely edible and not just non-toxic. However, sugar flowers are constructed with so many inedible components – wires, floristry tape, thread and stamens to name a few – that it is not so important that all the colours be edible.

### • Paste food colours

I use only a small selection of paste food colours for my flower making. I prefer to work with white or a very pale base colour and then create a stronger finished colour using powder food colours. I add paste colours into sugarpaste to cover the cakes – but even then I am not a huge fan of strongly coloured cake coverings. It is best to mix up a small amount of sugar- or flowerpaste with paste food colour, then add this smaller amount to a larger amount of paste – this prevents you adding too much colour to the entire amount of paste required – there's nothing worse than a screaming yellow cake!

### • Petal dusts

These are my favourite forms of food colour. These food colour dusts contain a gum which helps them to adhere to the petal or leaf. They are wonderful for creating very soft and also very intense colouring to finished flowers. It is this stage of flower making that gives me most satisfaction. The dusts can be mixed together to form different colours or brushed on in layers which I find creates more interest and depth to the finished flower or leaf. White petal dust can be added to soften the colours – some cake decorators add cornflour – however, this weakens the gum content of the dust, often causing a streaky effect to the petal. If you are trying to create strong, bold colours it is best to dust the surface of the flowerpaste while it is still fairly pliable or at the leather-hard stage. A paint can also be made by adding clear alcohol (iso-propyl) to the dust. This is good for adding spots and finer details. Another of my favourite uses of this dust is to add it to melted cocoa butter to make a paint that is wonderful for painting pictures and designs onto the surface of a cake – there are many examples of this technique in this book. Petal dusts can be used in small amounts to colour flowerpaste to create interesting subtle base colours.

### • Liquid colours

These are generally used to colour royal icing as they alter the consistency of flowerpaste, sugarpaste and almond paste but they can also be great to paint with. I use a small selection of liquid colour to paint fine spots and fine lines to petals. I mostly use cyclamen and poinsettia red liquid colours for flower making.

### • Craft dusts

These are inedible and only intended for items that are not going to be eaten – so perfect for flowers! Craft dusts are much stronger and much more light fast than food colour dusts. Care must be taken as they do tend to migrate the moment you take the lid of the pot. Dust in an enclosed space – once these colours go into the air they have a habit of landing where you don't want them to. To prevent spotty cakes it is best to keep the cake in a box while you are dusting the flowers, whether it is with craft or petal dusts.

### Glazing

Glazing can help give a leaf or a petal a more realistic appearance. Care must be taken not to glaze flowers too heavily as this can make them look very unnatural. The methods described below are different ways of glazing.

### • Steaming

Using powder colours on sugar flowers often leaves a slightly dry looking finished flower – this can be changed to create a slightly more waxy appearance and also to help set the colour to stop it leaving marks on the surface of the coated cake. Hold each flower in the steam from a boiling kettle for a few seconds, or until the surface turns slightly shiny. Take care not to scald yourself and also not to get the sugar too wet as it will dissolve fairly fast. Allow the flower to dry before wiring into a spray. If you are trying to create a velvety finish to a red rose for instance, then the steaming process can be used. You will then need to re-dust the flower. This technique will help an additional layer of dust to stick to the surface, giving the desired velvety effect.

### • Edible spray varnish

There are several ways to glaze leaves. Recently I have been using an edible spray varnish made by a company called Fabilo. This glaze can be used lightly for most leaves or sprayed in layers for shiny leaves and berries. You need to spray in a well-ventilated area and wear a filter mask. Spraying leaves is much quicker than the method below.

### • Confectioners' varnish

Confectioner's varnish creates a wonderful glossy finish for berries and some leaves. However, I mostly dilute confectioners' varnish with isopropyl alcohol – often sold in cake decorating shops as a glaze cleaner or dipping solution. I mix the two liquids together in a clean jam jar with a lid. Stir or swirl rather than shake the liquids to avoid producing air bubbles. Dip leaves into the glaze, shaking off the excess before hanging to dry or place onto kitchen paper to blot off any excess. The glaze can also be painted onto the leaf – but I find the bristles of the brush pull off some of the dust colour, producing a streaky effect. Watch the leaves as a build-up of glaze can give a very streaky shiny finish. I use various strengths of glaze: three-quarter glaze (one part isopropyl alcohol to three parts confectioners' varnish) gives a high glaze but takes away the plastic finish often left by undiluted confectioners' varnish; half glaze (equal proportions of the two) gives a natural shine for many types of foliage including ivy and rose leaves; and quarter glaze (three parts isopropyl alcohol to one part confectioners' varnish) is used for leaves and sometimes petals that don't require a shine but just need something stronger than just steaming to set the colour and remove the dusty finish.

# Recipes

*These recipes need no introduction – however, the editor required one so here it is! I have supplied a flowerpaste recipe but must admit that I always use a ready-made commercial paste (see suppliers).*

## Flowerpaste

Flowerpaste is used for making fine sugar flowers. It contains gum tragacanth, which helps to give it both stretch and strength. Though I have included a flowerpaste recipe, I prefer to buy it readymade mail order from a company called A Piece of Cake. Their paste gives much longer working time than most recipes and commercial pastes. The recipe below requires a heavy-duty mixer!

## Ingredients
*25 ml (5 tsp) cold water*
*10 ml (2 tsp) powdered gelatine*
*500 g (1 lb 2 oz /3 cups) icing sugar, sifted*
*15 ml (3 tsp) gum tragacanth*
*10 ml (2 tsp) liquid glucose*
*15 ml (3 tsp) white vegetable fat*
*1 medium free-range egg white*

**1** Mix the water and gelatine together in a small heatproof bowl and leave for 30 minutes. Sift the icing sugar and gum tragacanth into the bowl of a heavy-duty mixer.

**2** Place the bowl with the gelatine mixture over a small saucepan of hot water and stir until the gelatine has dissolved. Warm a teaspoon measure in hot water and then measure out the liquid glucose – the heat of the spoon should help ease the glucose off. Add the glucose and white vegetable fat to the gelatine mixture and continue to heat until everything has melted together. Stir.

**3** Add the dissolved mixture and the egg white to the icing sugar. Fit the beater to the machine and turn it on at its lowest speed, then gradually increase the speed to maximum until the paste becomes whiter and stringy.

**4** Remove the paste from the bowl and rub a very thin layer of white fat over it to prevent the surface drying out. Place in a plastic bag and store in an airtight container. Allow the paste to rest and mature for 12 hours or so before using it. Flowerpaste can be frozen but needs to be kneaded and put into a fresh plastic bag as the sugar crystals on the outer part of the paste tend to dry out the texture slightly.

## Royal icing

I have not used very much royal icing in this book, however, you might need some to attach ribbons to the base of a cake or you might prefer to pipe embroidery designs.

## Ingredients
*1 medium egg white (free-range and at*
*    room temperature)*
*225 g (8 oz / 1³/₄ cups) icing sugar, sifted*

**1** Wash the mixer bowl and the beater with a concentrated detergent and then scald to remove any traces of grease and left-over detergent.

**2** Place the egg white into the mixer bowl with most of the icing sugar and mix the two together with a spoon.

**3** Fix the bowl and beater to the machine and beat on the slowest speed for about 8 minutes until the icing has reached full peak. You might need to add a little extra icing sugar if the mixture is too soft.

## Cold porcelain

This is an inedible air-drying craft paste that can be used in almost exactly the same way as flowerpaste. The bonus with cold porcelain is that the flowers made from it are much stronger and less prone to breakages than those made from flowerpaste. However, because of its inedible nature, cold porcelain cannot come into direct contact with cakes and the flowers made from it need to be placed in a container. There are several commercial cold porcelain pastes available – the recipe below is the one that I prefer. Use measuring spoons and measuring cups to measure out the ingredients.

## Ingredients
*2¹/₂ Tbsp baby oil*
*¹/₂ cup (125 ml/4 fl oz) non-toxic hi-tack glue*
*    (Impex)*
*¹/₂ cup (125 ml/4 fl oz) white PVA wood glue*
*    (Liberon super wood glue or Elmers)*
*1 cup (125 g/4 oz) cornflour*
*Permanent white artists' gouache paint*

**1** Work in a well-ventilated area when making this paste. Wear a filter mask if you suffer from asthma. Measure the baby oil and the two types of glue together in a Teflon-coated saucepan to form an emulsion. Stir the cornflour into the mixture – it will go lumpy at this stage so don't worry!

**2** Place the pan over a medium heat and stir the paste with a heavy-duty plastic or wooden spoon. The paste will gradually come away from the base and the sides of the pan to form a ball around the spoon. Scrape any uncooked paste from the spoon and add to the mix. The cooking time will vary between gas, electric and ceramic hobs – the lower the heat and the slower you mix the paste, the smoother the resulting paste. I'm impatient so I tend to turn the heat up a little to cook faster (about 10 minutes, if that. A friend of mine misunderstood and cooked her paste on a very low heat for two hours – it was very, very smooth.) Keep on stirring the paste to cook evenly. You will need to split the paste and press the inner parts of the ball against the heat of the pan to cook it too – be careful not to overcook!

3 Turn the paste onto a non-stick board and knead until smooth. The kneading should help distribute some heat through the paste to cook any undercooked areas. If the paste is very sticky, you will need to cook it a little longer. It is better if it is slightly undercooked as you can always add heat later – if the paste is overcooked then it is almost impossible to work with.

4 Wrap in clingfilm and leave to cool – moisture will build up on the surface of the paste that if left will encourage mould growth so it is important to re-knead the paste when cool and then re-wrap it. Place in a plastic bag in an airtight container and store at room temperature. If stored correctly, this paste has been known to keep for two years.

5 Prior to making flowers you will need to add a smidge of permanent white gouache paint. The paste looks white but by its nature dries clear, giving a translucence to the finished flower. Adding the paint makes the finish more opaque. Handling the paste is quite similar to working with flowerpaste except I use cold cream cleanser instead of white vegetable fat, and glue or anti-bacterial wipes/water to moisten the petals to stick them. Cornflour is used as for flowerpaste. The paste shrinks a little as it dries – this is because of the glue. This can be disconcerting to begin with but you get used to it and it can be an advantage when making miniature flowers.

## Fruitcake

The smell of fruit soaking in alcohol and then being baked into a cake is one of my favourite aromas and this is my favourite fruitcake recipe – it is a variation of a recipe given to me by my friend Tombi Peck. Double the quantities for a three-tier wedding cake, plus line another small tin just in case there is some mixture left over. This recipe fills a 30-cm (12-in) square cake tin exactly (not that I ever make square cakes) or a 30-cm (12-in) round cake tin, with a little left over for a smaller cake. Even if I only need a 20-cm (8-in) oval cake I still make up this full quantity and bake extra cakes with the remaining mixture. The varieties and quantities of each dried fruit can be changed to suit your own taste – the original recipe contained currants, which I'm not a huge fan of, so I leave them out. When making this recipe, either use the imperial or metric measures, but don't mix the two.

## Ingredients

*1 kg (2 lb/8 cups) raisins*
*1 kg (2 lb/8 cups) sultanas*
*500 g (1 lb/4 cups) dried figs, chopped*
*500 g (1 lb/4 cups) dried prunes, chopped*
*250 g (8 oz/2 cups) natural colour glacée cherries, halved*
*125 g (4 oz/1 cup) dried apricots, chopped*
*125 g (4 oz/1 cup) dried or glacé pineapple, chopped*
*Grated zest and juice of 1 orange*
*200 ml (5 fl oz/$^1$/$_2$ cup) brandy (the odd dash of Cointreau or cherry brandy can be good too)*
*500 g (1 lb/2 cups) unsalted butter, at room temperature*
*250 g (8 oz/2 cups) light muscovado sugar*
*250 g (8 oz/2 cups) dark muscovado sugar*
*20 ml (4 tsp) apricot jam*
*40 ml (8 tsp) golden syrup*
*5 ml (1 tsp) each of ground ginger, allspice, nutmeg, cloves and cinnamon*
*2.5 ml ($^1$/$_2$ tsp) ground mace*
*500 g (1 lb/4 cups) plain flour*
*250 g (8 oz/1$^1$/$_2$ cups) ground almonds*
*10 large free-range eggs, at room temperature*

1 Halve and chop the various fruit that require it. Add or subtract the fruit accordingly to suit your taste but make sure the weight stays the same.

2 Mix the dried fruit, orange zest and juice, and alcohol together in a large plastic container with a lid. Seal and leave to soak for about a week or overnight will do.

3 Cream the butter in a large bowl until soft. Gradually add the sugars and beat the two together. Stir in the apricot jam, golden syrup, spices and mace.

4 Sieve the flour into a separate bowl and stir in the almonds. Beat the eggs together and add in batches to the butter/sugar mixture, alternating it with the flour/almond mix. Do not add the eggs too quickly as they might curdle.

5 Before you add the soaked fruit set aside a small amount of batter – this is used on top of the fruited batter to stop the fruit catching on the top in the oven. Mix the fruit into the remaining larger amount of batter. Grease and line the tin(s) with non-stick parchment. Fill with batter to the required depth – aim for about two-thirds the depth of the tin. Apply a thin layer of the un-fruited batter on top and smooth over.

6 Bake at a very low heat (gas 1/140°C/ 275°F) for 4–6 hours, depending on size. It is important to smell when the cake is ready as some ovens cook faster than others. The cake will shrink slightly from the side of the tin, be firm to the touch and smell wonderful. If in doubt test with a skewer – if it comes out clean the cake is ready.

7 Allow the cake to cool slightly in the tin, add a couple of extra dashes of alcohol and leave to cool further in the tin. Store wrapped in non-stick parchment and cling film. Allow to mature for as long as you have: a few days up to a few months.

# Flower build-ups

# Rosette succulent (Crassulaceae)

*These are made with several different succulents in mind! I love creating these wonderful fleshy forms of foliage as they need no cutters or veiners and are quick to make. The colour range includes soft pastel shades of blue, pink, purple and stronger red, almost black, foliage. Rosettes vary from 3 cm (1¹/₄ in) to more than 20 cm (8 in) wide.*

**METHOD**

I start these individual leaves small and gradually build them up to create a larger effect. I usually start to tape them into the rosette shape once I have made about ten leaves – I then decide if I need to continue to balance out the shape or add larger leaves.

1 Roll a ball of flowerpaste. Form it into a teardrop and insert a moistened white wire, the gauge of which will depend on the size of leaf being made. Work the paste at the base of the cone down onto the wire to form a 'neck'. Flatten the shape, carefully leaving a thicker area at the centre.

2 Soften the edges using the metal ball tool, then hollow the whole leaf. The pressure of the tool against the wire will create a central vein. Pinch the tip into a sharp point.

3 Tape the leaves together using quarter-width white floristry tape, gradually working up to using half-width tape.

4 Dust the rosette leaves and stem as a whole using layers of forest, foliage and edelweiss. Tinge the tips and edges as desired – I tend to use a mixture of plum and aubergine petal dusts. I have dusted the larger darker succulents with a vine green edge and used a mixture of aubergine, ruby and plum for the main areas. Glaze lightly using the edible spray varnish.

**Materials**

*Pale holly/ivy flowerpaste
26-, 28-, 30- and 33-gauge white wires
White floristry tape
Forest, foliage, edelweiss, plum, aubergine, vine green and ruby petal dusts*

**Equipment**

*Medium/large metal ball tool (Cc)
Edible spray varnish (Fabilo)*

# String of pearls and pumpkin seed succulents

*My friend Linda has a collection of over 300 types of cacti and succulent.*

*She introduced me to this wonderful, pretty evergreen succulent plant called*

*String of pearls/beads (Senecio rowleyanus) from South-East Africa.*

*It is very quick to create and requires minimum equipment.*

## STRING OF PEARLS

1 Cut several short lengths of very finest white wire you have. I like 35-gauge wire but it is not always easy to obtain. Roll small balls of well-kneaded pale green flowerpaste. Moisten the tip of the wires with fresh egg white and insert a single wire into each ball of paste. Pinch to secure the ball onto the wire – some of the leaves have a 'pinched' point too. Mark a 'window' onto each leaf using either a sharp scalpel or the plain-edge cutting wheel. Repeat to make leaves of various sizes. Allow to dry.

## ASSEMBLY AND COLOURING

2 The leaves can be dusted prior to assembly but I prefer to tape them onto a 33-gauge 'leader wire' using quarter-width nile green floristry tape and then dust the whole length of 'pearls' – it is a much quicker process. Leave a short stem to each of the individual leaves, alternating them down the stem and gradually increasing them in size as you go.

3 Use a light mixture of foliage, forest, edelweiss and vine green to dust the leaves. I tend to build up the colour gradually using a fairly large flat dusting brush for speed. Add tinges of aubergine petal dust if desired. Glaze very lightly using edible spray varnish.

## PUMPKIN SEED SUCCULENTS

4 These are made in a similar way to the 'string of pearls' – but this time think pumpkin seeds! There are pinched tips but no central vein here. Dust and glaze as in Step 3.

| Materials | Equipment |
|---|---|
| *33- and 35-gauge white wires* | *Sharp scalpel* |
| *Pale holly/ivy green flowerpaste* | *Plain-edge cutting wheel (PME)* |
| *Fresh egg white* | *Flat dusting brush* |
| *Foliage, forest, edelweiss, vine green and* | *Nile green floristry tape* |
| *aubergine petal dusts* | |
| *Edible spray varnish/glaze (Fabilo)* | |

# Rose-hips

*Rose-hips are great fun and very simple to make. Here I have chosen to wire*

*each sepal of the calyx, producing a much stronger finish. Vary the shape and*

*the colour of the hips as desired – I have made this version quite dark to work*

*with the red roses on my Everlasting love design on pages 126–27.*

### Materials

*Fine cotton lace maker's thread (120 gauge APOC)*
*24- and 33-gauge white wire*
*Very pale green flowerpaste*
*Black, nutkin brown, forest green, foliage, white,*
*aubergine, plum and ruby petal dusts*
*Edible spray varnish or full confectioner's glaze*

### Equipment

*Nile green floristry tape*
*Sharp scissors*
*Emery board*
*Calyx cutter (optional)*
*Rose leaf veiner (SKGI)*
*Small ball tool*
*Fine curved scissors*
*Fresh egg white*
*Pointed rose leaf cutters (J)*
*Briar rose leaf veiner*

## STAMENS

1 Wrap the fine cotton thread several times around two slightly parted fingers – the number of times the thread is wrapped will vary depending on the size of the hip and its stage of ripeness too! Remove the loop of thread from your fingers and twist it into a figure of eight shape and then fold the figure in half to produce a much smaller loop. Bend a length of 24-gauge wire through the centre of the loop and tape over tightly with half-width nile green floristry tape. Repeat this process at the opposite side of the loop to create two sets of stamens. Cut through the centre using sharp scissors. Trim shorter if required.

2 Rub the tips of the stamens against an emery board to 'fuzz-up' the tips giving a fluffy stamen-like finish. Dust the stamens with black and nutkin brown petal dusts. To create a more decayed look, hold the stamens over a naked flame to singe the tips slightly.

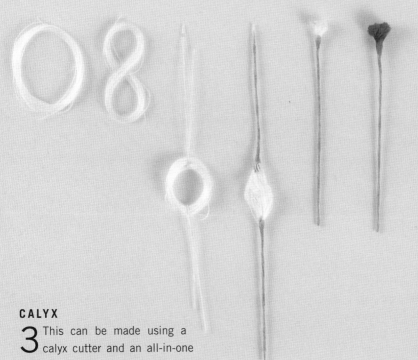

8 Dust the hip before the paste starts to dry. I have used plum, ruby and aubergine. Add tinges of foliage green, too. Allow to dry and then dip into a full strength confectioner's varnish – you will need to bend the stem up towards and past the tips of the calyx enabling you to dip the hip and avoid glazing the sepals.

## LEAVES

9 Follow the instructions on page 43 for the rose leaves. I have used pointed rose leaf cutters and a briar rose leaf veiner to texture the surface. If you are making the hips of the orange-red rosa rugosa, then you will need the black rose leaf set and the rosa rugosa leaf veiners as this variety has a specific rough texture that most other roses do not have.

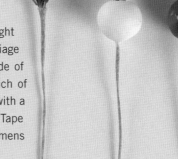

## CALYX

3 This can be made using a calyx cutter and an all-in-one method, however, I prefer to wire each sepal to give a stronger finish. Cut five short lengths of 33-gauge white wire. Attach a small ball of flowerpaste onto a dry wire and carefully roll and blend the paste onto the wire to create a long fine carrot shape tapering into a sharp point. Smooth the shape between your palms and place it onto the board to 'splat'/flatten it using the smooth side of the rose leaf veiner. If the shape is not exactly as you want it, then simply trim the sides into to shape using sharp scissors.

4 Place the sepal onto a pad or the palm of your hand and hollow out the length using a small ball tool – I tend to use a rolling action. Pinch the sepal from the base to the tip and curve it into shape.

5 Add 'hairy bits' to the edge using a fine pair of curved scissors to cut into the very edge. Flick the hairs back slightly. Repeat to make five sepals.

6 Dust each sepal with a light mixture of forest and foliage green petal dusts. Dust the inside of each sepal with white and a touch of the two greens. Catch the edges with a mixture of aubergine and plum. Tape the five sepals around the stamens using half-width nile green tape.

## HIP

7 The shape and size of the hip is up to you. I love the large round hips of roses like rosa rugosa. Roll a ball of pale green flowerpaste. Pull the wired calyx through the ball of paste using a small amount of fresh egg white to secure the two together. Pinch off any excess paste from the base of the hip.

# Mock orange

There are around 40 species of mock orange (Philadelphus) that take on shrub, tree or even climbing form. I have made a variety with fairly small white flowers with a pink tinge at the base of each petal. These are wonderful delicate flowers to use either by themselves or coupled with roses on wedding cakes.

### STAMENS

**1** At the heart of the stamens there is a pistil which I tend to omit from the flower – if you wish to add it then you will need to glue the length of four seed-head stamens (with their tips cut off) together. Leave the very ends un-glued and curl them back slightly. Tape or glue the pistil onto a 26-gauge wire. Allow to dry.

**2** Make small groups of white seed-head stamens and glue them together with non-toxic craft glue, working from the centre towards to tips. When dry, cut the stamens in half with scissors and trim away the excess stamen length to leave fairly short stamens. Glue these around the pistil and leave to dry. Dust the tips lightly with a mixture of daffodil, sunflower and white petal dusts. Dust the filaments of the stamens with vine green and white. Open up the stamens using a pair of fine tweezers.

| Materials | Equipment |
|---|---|
| White seed-head stamens | Scissors |
| Hi-tack non-toxic craft glue | Dusting brushes |
| Daffodil, sunflower, white, vine green, plum, foliage, forest and aubergine petal dusts | Fine tweezers |
| | Grooved board |
| White and pale holly/ivy flowerpaste | Christmas rose petal cutter (TT284) |
| 26-, 28-, 30- and 33-gauge white wires | Cupped Christmas rose petal veiner (SKGI) |
| Nile green floristry tape | Fuchsia sepal cutter (optional) |
| Edible spray varnish or quarter glaze (see page 11) | Philadelphus leaf veiners (SKGI) |
| | Plain-edge cutting wheel (PME) |
| | Fine curved scissors (optional) |
| | Dresden tool |

## PETALS

**3** Firstly, you will need to squash the cutter slightly to make a narrower petal shape. Thinly roll out some white flowerpaste onto the grooved board. Cut out four petals from the length of paste using the Christmas rose petal cutter. Insert a short 30-gauge white wire into the base of each petal. Soften the edges and vein using the cupped Christmas rose petal veiner. Pinch the petals at the base and at the tip. Allow to firm up a little before taping them onto the base of the stamens with half-width nile green floristry tape.

**4** Dust the base of each petal with plum petal dust.

## CALYX

**5** This can be made all in one with a fuchsia sepal cutter or, as I have done, wiring each individual sepal which gives more movement to the flower. Cut four short lengths of white 33-gauge wire. Roll a small ball of pale holly/ivy flowerpaste onto the end of the wire and work it into a long teardrop shape. Flatten the sepal with the flat side of the Philadelphus or cupped Christmas rose veiner. Pinch the sepal from the base to the tip. Repeat to make four sepals – two of them should be slightly longer in length.

**6** Tape the sepals onto the back of the flower. Add a small ball of pale holly/ivy flowerpaste just below the sepals to represent the ovary. Dust with a mixture of foliage and vine green.

## BUDS

**7** Cut short lengths of 33- or 30-gauge white wire. Bend hooks in the end of each. Form tiny cone shaped buds of white flowerpaste and insert a hooked wire into the base of each. Divide the surface into four using the plain-edge cutting wheel. Add a calyx as for the flower or create a quick cheat's calyx using a fine pair of curved scissors to cut four sepals from the main body of the bud. Twiddle the base of the calyx to create the ovary. Dust the calyx as described above for the flower.

## LEAVES

**8** Roll out some pale holly/ivy flowerpaste, leaving a thick ridge for the wire. Cut out a basic leaf shape using the plain-edge cutting wheel – mock orange can have very small or large, narrow or wide leaves depending on the variety you are making. Insert a 28- or 26-gauge wire into the ridge of the leaf.

**9** Create an open-toothed edge using the broad end of the dresden tool to pull out the paste at intervals from the edge of the leaf. Pinch the leaf to accentuate its central vein.

**10** Dust lightly with forest green and then more heavily with foliage and vine green. Add an edging of aubergine. Spray lightly with edible spray varnish or dip into a quarter glaze. Tape over each stem with quarter-width nile green floristry tape.

# Dissotis

*There are over 100 species of the African Dissotis, which can take on a creeping form or larger erect flowering shrubs. The flowers can be white, pink or purple.*

## STAMENS

**1** There are ten stamens in this flower; five are longer and fleshier than the other five. I have used short lengths of 36-gauge silk-covered wire to create both the long and short stamens. Add tiny amounts of white flowerpaste onto the end of each wire. Work the paste between your finger and thumb to form the anthers. Divide the length of each stamen using the plain-edge cutting wheel or sharp scalpel. Allow to dry.

**2** Paint the anthers with a mixture of deep magenta, deep purple and African violet craft dusts mixed with a little isopropyl alcohol. Tape them together with nile green floristry tape, positioning the heavier stamens so that they protrude further than the shorter, finer stamens. Curve the length of each stamen using a pair of fine-nose pliers or tweezers. Dust the length of the stamens with vine green petal dust.

## Materials

36-gauge silk-covered reel wire (Scientific wire company)

White and holly/ivy green flowerpaste (gumpaste)

Deep magenta, deep purple, vine green, African violet, plum, yellow, edelweiss, sap, aubergine, foliage and forest petal dusts

Isopropyl/glaze cleaner

Nile green floristry tape

26-, 28- and 30-gauge white wires

Hi-tack non-toxic glue

## Equipment

Fine-nose pliers or tweezers

Set of small rose petal cutters (TT277, 278)

Silk veining tool (HP)

Small calyx cutter (TT304, 526)

Medium/large metal ball tool (Cc)

Sage leaf cutters (TT852-855) (optional)

Tibouchina leaf veiners (SKGI)

Plain-edge cutting wheel (PME) or sharp scalpel

## PETALS

**3** Roll out some white flowerpaste to leave a thicker ridge down the centre for the wire – a grooved board may be used for this. Cut out the petal shape using one of the rose petal cutters – the size of the flower varies a little. Insert a moistened 30-gauge white wire into the thick ridge of the petal. Twiddle the base to elongate it slightly. Place the petal onto the board and vein using the silk veining tool to create fan formation veining.

**4** Place the petal over your index finger and frill the edge slightly using the silk veining tool again – be very careful not to dig the point of the tool down into the surface of the petal. Pinch the petal from the base to the tip. Curve slightly and allow to firm up a little before colouring. Repeat to make five petals.

## COLOURING AND ASSEMBLY

**5** Dust each petal with a mixture of African violet, plum and deep purple craft dusts. Add a touch of yellow and edelweiss at the base to highlight. If you are feeling brave, add some fine painted darker veins onto each petal using a mixture of isopropyl alcohol and the two purples (deep purple and African violet) used for the petals. Tape the five petals around the stamens using quarter-width nile green floristry tape.

## CALYX

**6** Roll out a small amount of green flowerpaste, leaving a thicker pimple at the centre. Cut out the calyx using one of the two sizes of calyx cutter – again this will depend on the size of the flower you have chosen to make. Soften the edges using the medium ball tool and a rolling action. Add a central vein to each sepal.

Thread the calyx onto the back of the flower using a little hi-tack glue to hold it in place behind the petals. Position a sepal in between each of the joins in the petals. Dust the calyx lightly with sap and vine green petal dusts.

## FOLIAGE

**7** Roll out some more green flowerpaste, leaving a thick ridge for the wire. Cut out the leaf shape using one of the four sizes of sage leaf cutter. Insert a 28- or 26-gauge white wire into the ridge. Soften the edge and vein using the Tibouchina leaf veiner. Pinch the leaf from the base to the tip to accentuate the central vein. The leaves grow in pairs.

**8** Dust with aubergine on the edges of the leaves. Over dust with a mixture of foliage, forest, edelweiss and vine green. Steam carefully to give the leaf a slight glaze.

# Rothmania

*There are about twenty species of Rothmania from tropical and South Africa. The length of the back of the flower varies between species and the flowers can be white, creamy-white or with wonderful dark brown-aubergine coloured backs.*

### STAMENS

1 Cut five lengths of 33-gauge wire. Attach a small ball of white flowerpaste onto the end of a dry wire and work the paste down the wire to form a slender sausage shaped anther. Mark a line down the length using the plain-edge cutting wheel. Repeat to make five stamens. Dust the anthers with a light mixture of daffodil, sunflower and white petal dusts. Dust the length (filament) of the stamen with vine green.

### PISTIL

2 Roll a small ball of holly/ivy flowerpaste and insert a 26-gauge wire. Work the paste down the wire with your finger and thumb to create a long, slender pistil. Flatten the tip slightly and pinch it to form a small bead shape. Pinch the tip with tweezers to create three sections. Dust lightly with vine green petal dust. Tape the stamens around the pistil using half-width nile green floristry tape. Position them so that they are slightly shorter than the pistil. Add an extra 22-gauge wire to the base of the stamens to create a stronger stem for the flower.

**Materials**

*18-, 22-, 24, 26- and 33-gauge white wires*
*White and holly/ivy flowerpaste*
*Daffodil, sunflower, white, vine green, aubergine, foliage green and forest petal dusts*
*Nile green floristry tape*
*Fresh egg white*
*Cyclamen liquid food colour (SK)*
*Edible spray varnish*

**Equipment**

*Plain-edge cutting wheel (PME)*
*Fine tweezers*
*Celstick*
*Smooth ceramic tool (HP)*
*Petunia cutter (TT435)*
*Sharp curved scissors*
*Grooved board (optional)*
*Large gardenia leaf veiner (SKGI)*
*Fine paintbrush*

## FLOWER

**3** Form a ball of well-kneaded white flowerpaste into a long slender carrot shape. Pinch out the broad end using your fingers and thumbs to create a 'wizard' hat shape. Place onto a non-stick board and roll out the 'brim' with the celstick or smooth ceramic tool to make it slightly thinner – although remember this needs to be a fairly fleshy flower. Place the petunia cutter over the pedicel and cut out the flower shape, scrubbing the cutter and paste against the board to create a clean-cut edge. Remove the flower from the cutter.

**4** Using a rolling action, broaden each of the petals using the celstick or smooth ceramic tool – start from the centre of each petal working out either edge and leaving a central vein slightly thicker down the length of the petal.

**5** Open up the throat of the flower using the pointed end of the smooth ceramic tool. Press the tool against the inner throat of the flower, working it against your fingers to thin it slightly. Pinch a light central vein down each petal. Moisten the base of the stamen wires with fresh egg white and thread them through the centre of the flower. Thin down the back of the flower if required.

**6** Create a quick calyx by snipping into the base of the flower with curved scissors to create five sepals. Pinch each sepal between your finger and thumb to soften the cut shape slightly. Mark a line between each sepal using the plain-edge cutting wheel.

## BUD

**7** Use half length 26- or 24-gauge wire, depending on the size of bud you are making. Insert the wire into a cone shape of white paste. Thin down the base of the cone to work it down the length of the wire to create the long characteristic bud shape. Divide the tip into five petals using the plain-edge cutting wheel. Twist the petals slightly. Snip a calyx as for the flower.

## LEAVES

**8** Roll out some holly/ivy flowerpaste, leaving a thick ridge for the wire – you may prefer to use a grooved board for this. Cut out a basic leaf shape using the plain-edge cutting wheel. Insert a moistened 26- or 24-gauge wire into the thick ridge of the leaf so that it supports about half the length of the leaf. Soften the edges and vein using the large gardenia leaf veiner. Pinch the length of the leaf to accentuate the central vein.

## COLOURING AND ASSEMBLY

**9** Paint fine spots onto the flower using a fine paintbrush and cyclamen liquid food colour. Dust the back of the flower and buds heavily with aubergine petal dust. Colour the snipped calyx with foliage green. Dust the leaves in layers with vine green, forest and foliage. Tinge the edges with aubergine. Spray lightly with edible spray varnish.

**10** Tape a couple of smaller leaves onto the end of an 18-gauge wire using half-width nile green floristry tape. Add a bud to hang down the stem and add one, two or three leaves where the bud joins the main stem. Continue adding buds and flowers, alternating their position as you add them. Dust the main stem with aubergine petal dust.

# Akebia

This pretty ornamental climber is a native of Japan, Korea and China. The more common species is of a chocolate-aubergine colour and is often known as the chocolate vine. In fact, the flowers have a slightly spiced almost chocolate vanilla scent to them. There are many hybrid forms, including a white chocolate variety. I have chosen a pretty pink hybrid for this project. The foliage can be in sets of five or three, depending on the variety. The plant sometimes produces an unusual edible fruit with a jelly-like flesh — not much taste to it but interesting all the same.

## Materials

*33-gauge white wire*
*Pale pink and pale holly/ivy flowerpaste*
*Nile green floristry tape*
*Plum, African violet, aubergine, forest,*
*foliage and vine green petal dusts*
*Edible spray varnish (Fabilo)*

## Equipment

*Scissors*
*Tweezers*
*Sharp scalpel*
*Plain-edge cutting wheel (PME)*
*Tulip cutters (TT137, 171)*
*Non-stick board*
*Celstick*
*Ball tool*
*Dusting brush*
*Grooved board*
*Australian rose petal cutters (TT349–352)*
*Briar rose leaf veiner (SKGI)*
*Curved scissors*

### STAMENS

1 To make the stamens for the female flower cut six short lengths of 33-gauge white wire. Attach a small ball of pink flowerpaste to the end of one of the dry wires. Work the paste into a cigar shape onto the wire using your finger and thumb. Flatten the tip of the stamen with your fingers. Pinch the end with tweezers three times to give a slight trefoil shape. Repeat to make six stamens and then tape them together with quarter-width nile green floristry tape.

2 For the smaller flowers I attach a small ball of pale pink flowerpaste onto the end of a hooked 33-gauge wire and divide the surface into six sections using either a sharp scalpel or plain-edge cutting wheel.

## OUTER BRACTS

**3** It is easier to make these bracts using a trefoil-shaped tulip petal cutter. Roll out a small amount of pale pink flowerpaste onto the non-stick board using a celstick and leaving a raised pimple at the centre. Cut out the shape using one of the two sizes of tulip cutters.

**4** Soften the edges of each section using a ball tool and then hollow out the centre of each section to create three cupped bracts.

**5** Mark a few lines onto each bract using the small end of the plain-edge cutting wheel.

**6** Moisten the base of the stamens and thread them through the centre of the trefoil bract shape. Pinch the pimple behind the flower to help secure it in place. You might need to dry the flower upside down for a while to allow the bracts to firm up a little. Repeat to make several. Use the smaller tulip cutter to attach bracts to the small sets of stamens. Allow to dry before dusting.

## COLOURING AND ASSEMBLY

**7** Dust each flower with plum and then tinges of African violet. Keep the smaller flowers much paler in colour. Tape the flowers into groups using quarter-width nile green floristry tape. Keep some groups just with small flowers and some with small and large together. Steam gently to set the colour.

## LEAVES

These can be in sets of three or five depending on the variety of Akebia. I prefer sets of five. The Australian rose petal cutters will need to be squashed to make the leaves narrower in shape.

**8** Roll out some pale holly/ivy coloured flowerpaste, leaving a thick ridge for the wire – a grooved board can be used successfully for these small leaves. Cut out a leaf shape using one of the Australian rose petal cutters. Insert a short length of moistened 33-gauge wire into the thick ridge of the leaf. Soften the edges with a ball tool and vein using the briar rose leaf veiner.

**9** Pinch the leaf from the base to the tip. Some varieties have leaves with a slight indent to the tip – if you want to create this effect simply trim into the tip of the leaf with curved scissors to form a tiny 'V'-shaped cut. Repeat to make five leaves – one large, two smaller and two smaller again for each set.

**10** Tape over each individual leaf stem with quarter-width nile green floristry tape and then tape the five leaves together into a hand/fan formation, leaving a little of each taped stem showing. Repeat to make a variety of sizes.

**11** Dust the edges of each leaf with aubergine and plum petal dusts mixed together. Dust the main bulk of the leaf in layers of forest, foliage and vine green. Keep the backs pale. Spray lightly with edible spray varnish.

# Tweedia

*The pretty blue flowers of this*
*South American woody twining*
*shrub are great to add to*
*bouquets where a true blue*
*flower is required. Its Latin*
*name is a bit of a mouthful –*
*Oxypetalum caeruleum!*

### Materials

*22-, 26-, 28-, 30- and 33-gauge white wires*
*White, pale blue and pale holly/ivy flowerpaste*
*Ultramarine craft dust*
*White, African violet and foliage petal dusts*
*Edible spray varnish (Fabilo)*
*Nile green floristry tape*

### Equipment

*Plain-edge cutting wheel (PME)*
*Smooth ceramic tool (HP)*
*Tweedia flower cutter (AD) or stephanotis cutter*
*Sharp curved scissors*
*Grooved board (optional)*
*Tweedia leaf cutters (AD),*
*or see template on page 141*
*Sharp scalpel (optional)*
*Briar rose leaf veiner (SKGI)*

## STAMEN AND COROLLA

**1** Cut a length of 26-gauge white wire into thirds. Roll a tiny ball of white flowerpaste and insert a moistened wire into it. Form the ball into a teardrop shape. Mark a few lines down the length of it using the plain-edge cutting wheel to represent fused stamens. Allow to dry.

**2** Take a very small ball of pale blue flowerpaste and form it into a cone shape. Hollow and thin out the centre of the cone using the pointed end of the smooth ceramic tool. Moisten the base of the stamen and pull through the centre of the corolla. Allow to dry.

## FLOWER

**3** Form a teardrop-shaped piece of very pale blue flowerpaste. Pinch out the broad end of the shape and pinch to form a 'hat' shape. Place the shape onto a non-stick board and roll out the 'brim' of the hat using the smooth ceramic tool. Try to keep the main body of the shape fairly slim.

**4** Place the tweedia or stephanotis cutter over the thick centre to cut out the flower shape. Pick up the cutter with the shape still stuck in it and rub over the edges with your fingers to remove any rough edges to the petals. Push the shape through the cutter from the flat side using the ceramic tool.

**5** Place the flower flat-side down against the board and using the smooth ceramic tool roll each of the petals to elongate them slightly. Pick up the flower and open up its throat using the pointed end of the tool.

**6** Pinch each petal from the back to create an attractive shape. Moisten the base of the corolla and pull through the centre of the flower. Pinch from behind the flower to secure them together.

**7** Create a quick calyx by snipping into the base of the flower five times with a sharp pair of curved scissors.

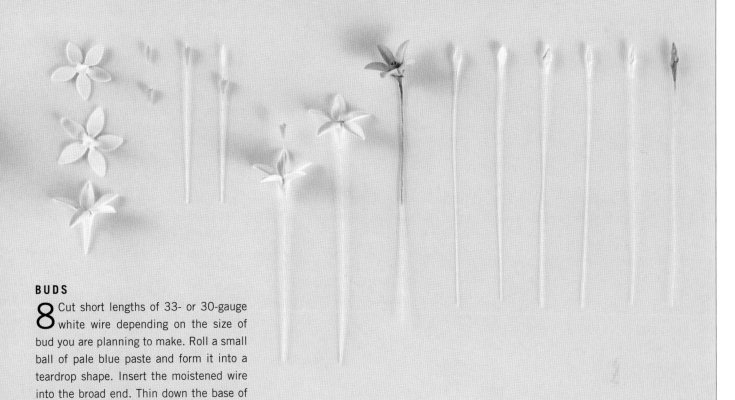

## BUDS

**8** Cut short lengths of 33- or 30-gauge white wire depending on the size of bud you are planning to make. Roll a small ball of pale blue paste and form it into a teardrop shape. Insert the moistened wire into the broad end. Thin down the base of the bud to create a short neck. Pinch three petals from the tip of the bud. Twist them around to create a spiralled effect. Snip into the base to create the calyx as for the flower.

## LEAVES

**9** Roll out some pale holly/ivy flowerpaste leaving a thick ridge for the wire (a grooved board may also be used to speed up this process). Cut out the leaf shape using one of the tweedia leaf cutters or with a template and a sharp scalpel.

**10** Insert a moistened 28- or 26-gauge white wire into the thick ridge of the leaf. Soften the edges and vein using the briar rose leaf veiner. The leaves occur in pairs. Smaller leaves can be made using the quicker method of wiring fine teardrop-shaped pieces of holly/ivy paste onto fine wires – 30- or 33-gauge. Flatten the teardrop using the flat side of the veiner and then vein using the textured sides of the briar rose veiner. Pinch each leaf from the base to the tip to create a little character.

## DUSTING AND ASSEMBLY

**11** Dust the flower and buds with a light mixture of ultramarine craft dust, and white and African violet petal dusts. Use a darker mixture (with less white) to colour the corolla. Dust the calyx with foliage and white mixed together. Dust the leaves with foliage and a little white petal dust. Add some of the flower colour to the edges of the leaves. Spray lightly with edible spray varnish.

**12** Tape two tiny leaves together at the end of a 22-gauge wire using half-width nile green floristry tape. Continue to add and graduate the size of the leaves as you work down the stem. Add buds and flowers in twos or threes at the junction of each pair of leaves.

# Dancing ladies ginger

*I was so pleased to find that this plant has such a pretty common name – its botanical name, which I have a soft spot for too, is Globba! The tiny yellow flowers of this plant are very complex to make – I have chosen to use only buds! It is the bright pink, sometimes white, bracts of the plant that create such a delicate effect to sprays and arrangements.*

### Materials

*26-, 28-, 30- and 33-gauge wire*
*White and pink flowerpaste*
*Sunflower, daffodil, foliage green, vine green, plum and African violet petal dusts*
*Nile green floristry tape*

### Equipment

*Curved scissors*
*Stargazer B petal veiner (SKGI)*
*or cupped Christmas rose veiner (SKGI)*

### BUDS

**1** Cut short lengths of 33-gauge white wires. Attach a tiny ball of white flowerpaste onto the end of the wire and roll the base to form a slight neck to the bud. Cut into the base of the bud with curved scissors to represent the calyx – I aim for five cuts but some of the smaller ones only get three. Repeat to make several buds in varying sizes.

**2** Dust with sunflower and daffodil petal dusts. Dust the calyx and the stem with a mixture of vine green and foliage green.

### BRACTS

**3** Cut short lengths of 33-, 30- or 28-gauge wire, depending on the size of bract you are making. Work a small ball of pink flowerpaste onto the wire and form it into a rounded cone shape. Smooth the cone in your palms.

**4** Flatten the cone against a non-stick board using the flat side of the Stargazer B veiner or the cupped Christmas rose veiner. Soften the edges if required and then vein using the Stargazer B veiner. Repeat to make varying sizes. Pinch each bract down the centre and curve back slightly.

**5** Dust with plum petal dust. Add tinges of African violet, too, if desired. For the white variety, dust the base of the bracts with vine green.

**6** Tape the bracts onto a 26-gauge wire using half-width nile green floristry tape. Add the buds as you work, positioning them from the base of the bracts. Bend the stem to create delicate shapes.

# Kumquat

*Kumquats are very closely related to the more familiar* Citrus *family, however, they belong to the genus* Fortunella. *In fact, the flowers of the plant are very similar. These cute fruit are a great addition to any arrangement and bouquet, being both simple and quick to make.*

## FRUIT

**1** Roll a ball of well-kneaded pale vine green flowerpaste. Form the ball into a longer egg shape. Insert a hooked moistened 24- or 22-gauge wire into the slimmer end of the fruit. Pinch the paste to secure it firmly to the wire.

**2** Texture the surface by rolling the fruit against a fine nutmeg grater. Use the flat end of a cocktail stick to create an indent at the tip of the fruit.

**3** Snip a quick calyx into the base of the fruit using sharp curved scissors.

**4** Dust in layers depending upon the ripeness you are trying to create with vine green, tangerine and red. Dust the calyx with a mixture of foliage and forest. Allow to dry, then spray with edible spray glaze.

## LEAVES

**5** Roll out some holly/ivy green flowerpaste leaving a thick ridge for the wire. Cut out the leaf shape using the pointed end of the simple leaf cutter as the base of the leaf. You will need to use the four sizes of cutter to create a selection of foliage.

**6** Insert a moistened 28-gauge wire into the thick ridge. Soften the edges and vein using a lightly textured rose leaf or fresh citrus leaf. Pinch the central vein slightly.

**7** Dust the leaves darker on the front than the back with foliage, vine and forest green. Allow to dry. Lightly glaze with spray varnish and tape over the foliage and fruit with quarter-width nile green floristry tape.

### Materials
*Pale vine green and holly/ivy flowerpaste*
*22-, 24- and 28-gauge white wire*
*Vine, tangerine, red, foliage and forest petal dusts*
*Edible spray varnish*
*Nile green floristry tape*

### Equipment
*Small nutmeg grater*
*Flat-headed cocktail sticks*
*Sharp curved scissors*
*Simple leaf cutters (TT229-232)*
*Fine textured rose leaf or*
*fresh citrus leaf*

# Polyalthia

*A genus of 120 species from South East Asia, sometimes called 'Pisang-pisang'. The plant takes the form of a tree with colourful fragrant flowers that produce reddish-black berries when fully ripe.*

### Materials
*26-, 28- and 33-gauge white wires*
*White and pale holly/ivy flowerpaste*
*White and nile green floristry tape*
*Vine green, white, plum, coral, forest, foliage and aubergine petal dusts*
*Edible spray varnish*

### Equipment
*Stargazer B petal veiner (SKGI)*
*Fine tweezers*
*Plain-edge cutting wheel (PME)*
*Gardenia leaf veiner (SKGI)*

## PETALS

1 Cut two lengths of 33-gauge white wire into thirds to make six shorter lengths of wire. Take a very small ball of white paste and wrap it around the end of the wire blending and elongating it with your finger and thumb. Form the petal into a point at the tip.

2 Place the narrow petal down against the board and flatten it using the flat side of the Stargazer B petal veiner. Next, vein the petal using the veined sides of the Stargazer B veiner. Pinch the petal from the base to the tip to accentuate the central vein. Repeat to make six petals. Curve each slightly.

## PISTIL

3 The pistil and stamens have been simplified for my version of this flower. Attach a tiny ball of white flowerpaste onto the end of a 28-gauge wire and form into a cone shape. Pinch the cone with tweezers to texture the surface. Allow to dry.

4 Tape the six petals around the pistil using quarter-width white floristry tape. If the petals are still pliable reshape them if required. Form a long back to the flower by adding a ball of white flowerpaste working it into the base of the petals with your finger and thumb and then work the paste down the stem. Smooth the paste between your palms. Curve the back of the flower.

## BUDS

5 Form a cone of white flowerpaste. Insert a 26-gauge wire into the base. Thin down the back of the bud to create an elongated neck. Divide the tip of the bud into six using the plain-edge cutting wheel. Twist the petals slightly. Curve as for the flower.

6 Dust the buds and flowers lightly with a mixture of vine green and white petal dusts. Add tinges of plum and coral mixed together to the tips of the buds, back of the flowers and base of each flower petal.

## LEAVES

7 These are made with a pale holly/ivy coloured flowerpaste and cut out using the plain-edge cutting wheel. The leaves are wired onto 26-gauge wire and veined with the gardenia leaf veiner. Dust in layers with forest, foliage and vine green petal dusts. Add light tinges of aubergine. Glaze lightly with spray varnish.

# $\mathcal{P}$aphia

*This Fijian plant is one of about
fifteen species that are found scattered
in New Guinea, Queensland and Fiji.
It is a shrub or small tree and some
small plants take an epiphytic form.*

## PISTIL AND STAMENS

**1** Attach a tiny ball of pale holly/ivy paste onto the end of a short length of 33-gauge wire. Form a tiny bead of paste at the tip of the pistil and thin down the base to elongate it. Glue together small bunches of stamens at the centre using non-toxic craft glue – leave either end of the stamens un-glued. Cut the stamens in half and cut down the length a little, too. Attach the short groups around the pistil using extra glue. Allow to dry. Dust the stamens with sunflower and daffodil petal dusts. Dust the pistil with vine green.

## FLOWER

**2** Form a ball of pale melon flowerpaste into a long pedicel. Thin out the base of the shape against a non-stick board, using the celstick to roll out the paste. The back of the flower is too heavy to fit into the calyx cutter shape, so to cut out the shape it is easier to place the flower on top of the cutter and roll the paste against the cutter using the celstick.

**3** Open up the throat of the flower using the pointed end of the celstick. Vein and broaden each petal using the silk veining tool. Thread the stamens through the throat of the flower.

**4** Create the hip of the calyx using a cocktail stick to roll against the base of the flower shape forming a division 'waistline'. Snip five sepals using curved scissors into the main section of the flower back to join them up against the 'waistline'.

**5** Dust the back of the flower with tangerine. The edges of the calyx are dusted with vine green and then the main hip of the calyx and the petals are dusted with a mixture fuchsia and plum. Glaze the calyx of the flower using a light spray of edible spray varnish.

## LEAVES

**6** Roll out some pale holly/ivy paste leaving a thick ridge for the wire. Cut out the leaf shape using a sharp scalpel or plain-edge cutting wheel. Insert a moistened 26-gauge wire into the ridge. The edges of the leaf are unevenly toothed; use a sharp scalpel to cut into the edge of the leaf – flick the blade into and away from the leaf to create this effect. Vein using the briar rose leaf veiner. Pinch the leaf to accentuate the central vein. Dust with vine green and foliage petal dusts. Glaze lightly with edible spray varnish.

**Materials**

*Pale melon and pale holly/ivy flowerpaste*
*26- and 33-gauge wire*
*Fine white or yellow stamens*
*Non-toxic craft glue (Impex)*
*Sunflower, daffodil, vine green, tangerine, fuchsia,*
*    plum and foliage petal dusts*
*Edible spray varnish*

**Equipment**

*Celstick*
*Calyx cutter (TT526)*
*Silk veining tool (HP)*
*Cocktail stick*
*Sharp curved scissors*
*Sharp scalpel*
*Plain-edge cutting wheel (PME)*
*Briar rose leaf veiner (SKGI)*

33

# Hawaiian swinging pea

*I have renamed this plant! Both its Latin name, Strongylodon, and native name, nukuiiwii, are real mouthfuls. Its native Hawaiian name is derived from 'nuku', meaning beak, and 'iiwi', a native red-feathered bird with a curved bill. In days gone by the Hawaiians used the strong pliable stems of the plant as swings!*

### BUDS

**1** You will need to make some of these buds on 33-gauge wire and the larger buds on 30-gauge wire. Some of the larger beak-like buds can be used as the centre for the flower. Form a small cone shape of coral flowerpaste. Insert a short length of moistened wire into the rounded end. Thin down the rounded end against the wire to form a more elongated shape. Pinch, flatten and curve the shape slightly to form a slight crescent shape. With the plain-edge cutting wheel, mark a single line on the back of the larger buds that are intended to be finished as flowers – these are used to represent the 'keel' at the centre of the flower.

### INNER PETALS

**2** Roll out some coral flowerpaste and cut out one petal shape using the Australian rose petal cutter. Cut the petal in half using a sharp scalpel or plain-edge cutting wheel to make two narrow petals. Use the rose petal cutter again to re-cut the straight edge on each petal left by the division or alternatively trim the edge to create a more rounded finish using a pair of sharp, curved scissors.

**3** Vein each of the petals using the silk veining tool and then hollow out the centre of each petal using a small ball tool. Attach the two petals onto either side of the keel using a small amount of egg white. You will need to hang this section upside down for a while to help the petals set in place on the keel.

**Materials**
22-, 26-, 28-, 30- and 33-gauge white wires
Pale coral and holly/ivy flowerpaste
Egg white
Coral, red, ruby, aubergine, sunflower, foliage and vine green petal dusts
Nile green floristry tape
Edible spray varnish

**Equipment**
Australian rose petal cutter (TT350)
Sharp scalpel or plain-edge cutting wheel (PME)
Sharp, curved scissors
Ceramic silk veining tool (HP)
Small ball tool
Dusting brushes
Hydrangea leaf veiner (SKGI)

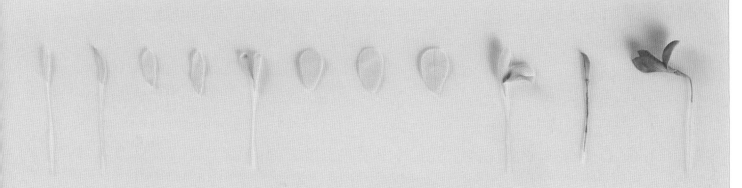

## STANDARD (OUTER) PETAL

**4** Roll out some more coral flowerpaste and cut out another rose petal shape using the rose petal cutter. Vein in a fan formation using the silk veining tool. Pinch a central vein down the centre of the petal. Attach to the back of the first two petals on the keel. Dry slightly in a hanging position to allow the paste to firm up slightly before starting to curl the petal back slightly. Allow to dry a little more before dusting.

## CALYX

**5** I have created a quick calyx to the buds and flowers simply by adding a tiny ball of holly/ivy flowerpaste at the base of each and snipped into it five times using a pair of curved scissors.

## DUSTING AND ASSEMBLY

**6** Dust each flower and bud in layers, starting with coral and then a touch of red and ruby petal dusts. Dust the calyx and stem with aubergine. Add a touch of sunflower into the base of the standard petal.

**7** Start taping the small buds together onto a 26-gauge wire, gradually increasing the buds in size as you create a trailing stem. Add the flowers towards the base of the stem.

## LEAVES

**8** These grow in sets of three – one large and two smaller on either side. Roll out some pale holly/ivy flowerpaste, leaving a thick ridge for the wire. Cut out a fairly rounded leaf shape using the plain-edge cutting wheel. Insert a 28- or 26-gauge wire into the ridge, depending on the size of the leaf.

**9** Soften the edge with a ball tool, then vein using the hydrangea leaf veiner. Pinch the leaf to accentuate the central vein. Leave to dry for a short while and then tape over each leaf stem with nile green floristry tape and then into their sets of three.

**10** Dust in layers with foliage and vine green. Add a little aubergine to the edges. Spray with edible spray varnish.

**11** Tape the flower stems and foliage onto a 22-gauge wire using half-width nile green tape. Add a set of foliage where the flower stem grows out of the main stem. Dust the stems with aubergine and foliage.

# Coffee

*Several years ago my friend Tombi and I made a video of how to make flowers – it was called 'The Fruity Video by the Nuts'! We made various flowers, fruit and nuts during the half hour-long live demonstration – amongst them Tombi created coffee flowers and their cherries – this is my take on her original version. To our relief the video is no longer available!!!*

### Materials
20, 26-gauge white wires
Nile green and white floristry tape
White and holly/ivy flowerpaste
Small white seed-head stamens
Cream, vine green, white, daffodil,
foliage, red, ruby, aubergine and
forest, petal dusts
Edible spray varnish (Fabilo)

### Equipment
Sharp scissors
Cocktail stick
Dusting brush
Non-stick board
Smooth ceramic tool (HP) or celstick
Large stephanotis cutter (TT)
Plain-edge cutting wheel (PME)
Piping tubes: no. 2 and no. 3
Large gardenia leaf veiner (SKGI)

## PISTIL AND STAMENS

**1** Tape the end of a 26-gauge wire with quarter-width white floristry tape leaving a flap of tape about 1.5 cm (½ in) above the wire. Cut the flap in half lengthways and curl the ends away from one another with a cocktail stick.

**2** Cut the tips off five stamens. Roll five very fine strands of white flowerpaste to create the anthers. Insert a stamen into each strand. Pinch and angle the anther slightly to hold them in place. Allow to dry. Tape the stamens around the pistil using quarter-width white floristry tape. Dust the anthers with cream petal dust.

## FLOWER

**3** Form a ball of well-kneaded white flowerpaste into a cone shape. Pinch the broad end of the cone to create a hat shape. Place against the non-stick board and thin out the base using the smooth ceramic tool or celstick. Cut out the flower shape by placing the stephanotis cutter over the 'neck' and press firmly against the board. Pick up the flower and the cutter (it will be stuck in the cutter at this stage) and rub your thumb over the edge of the cutter to create a clean-cut edge. Push out the flower using the ceramic tool.

**4** Elongate each petal slightly using the ceramic tool. Open up the throat of the flower with the pointed end of the tool.

**5** Hollow out the back of each petal and pinch them backwards at the tips. Thread the stamens through the flower and firmly work the back of the flower onto the wire to secure the two together. Cut away and remove any excess paste that might have been created during this process.

Dust the base with vine green and white mixed together. Add a touch of vine green, white and daffodil mixed together into the throat of the flower.

### BUD

**6** Form a cone-shaped piece of white flowerpaste. Insert a moistened 26-gauge wire into the broad end of the cone. Thin down the broad base onto the wire to create a longer neck. Divide the bud into five sections using the plain-edge cutting wheel. Twist the bud slightly. Dust the base with a light mixture of white and vine green petal dusts.

### COFFEE CHERRIES

**7** Roll a ball of pale holly/ivy flowerpaste and form it into a slight barrel shape. Insert a hooked wire into the base and pinch to secure it in place. Mark two circles on the tip of the fruit using a no. 2 and then no. 3 piping tubes.

**8** Dust the cherries to create a ripening effect, starting with a mixture of vine green and foliage, gradually adding tinges of red through to strong red tinged with ruby and strong ruby tinged with aubergine. Allow to dry and spray with edible spray varnish.

### LEAVES

**9** Roll out some holly/ivy flowerpaste leaving a thick ridge. Cut out a freehand leaf using the plain-edge cutting wheel. Insert a moistened 26-gauge wire into the ridge so that it supports about half the length of the leaf. Soften the edge using a metal ball tool.

**10** Vein firmly using the large gardenia leaf veiner. Pinch the leaf from the base to the tip to accentuate its central vein. Make leaves of various sizes. They tend to grow in pairs and sets of three – I often use the leaves singularly to create attractive tapered stems.

**11** Dust in layers of forest, foliage and vine green. Allow to dry and then glaze lightly with spray varnish.

# Auricula

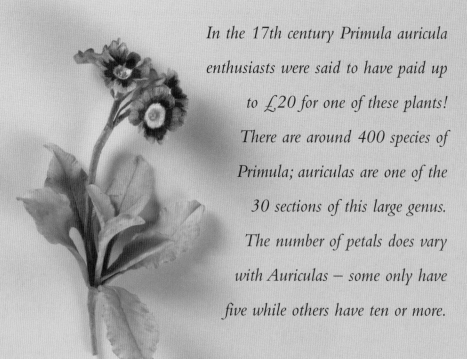

*In the 17th century Primula auricula enthusiasts were said to have paid up to £20 for one of these plants! There are around 400 species of Primula; auriculas are one of the 30 sections of this large genus. The number of petals does vary with Auriculas — some only have five while others have ten or more.*

## Materials

*26- and 28-gauge white wire*
*Pale holly/ivy and white flowerpaste*
*Hi-tack non-toxic craft glue*
*White seed-head stamens*
*Vine green, white, daffodil, sunflower, plum,*
*aubergine, coral, foliage, bluegrass and*
*forest petal dusts*
*Cyclamen liquid colour (SK)*
*Edible spray varnish*
*Nile green floristry tape*

## Equipment

*Sharp scissors*
*Fine paintbrush and larger dusting brushes*
*Smooth ceramic tool (HP)*
*Banks rose cutters (TT662–664)*
*Silk veining tool*
*Plain-edge cutting wheel*
*Dresden veining tool*
*Primrose leaf cutters (TT564, 565)*
*Ball tool*
*Hellebore leaf veiner (ALDV)*

## PISTIL AND STAMENS

1 Cut a 26-gauge wire into thirds. Attach a tiny ball of pale holly/ivy flowerpaste onto the end of a wire. Form the pistil leaving a tiny bead at the tip. Allow to dry. Glue together three white seed-head stamens from the centre to just below the tips with non-toxic craft glue. Allow to set. Cut the stamens in half and trim away the excess to leave two short sets of stamens. Apply a little more glue and attach to the wire around the pistil. Dust the pistil very lightly with a mix of vine green and white petal dusts. Dust the tips of the stamens with daffodil and sunflower mixed together.

## FLOWER

2 Form a ball of white flowerpaste into a teardrop shape and pinch out the broad end to form a hat shape. Thin out the brim of the hat using the smooth ceramic tool against a non-stick board. Cut out the flower shape with one of the three sizes of banks rose cutters – I have used the medium-sized cutter for the flowers in this project.

3 Broaden each petal, leaving a central ridge down the centre with the silk veining tool. Open up the centre using the pointed end of the smooth ceramic tool and add a little texture with the tool on the front of the petals. Pinch each petal down the centre from behind to accentuate a central vein.

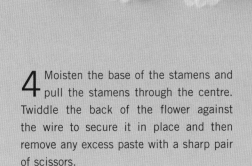

**4** Moisten the base of the stamens and pull the stamens through the centre. Twiddle the back of the flower against the wire to secure it in place and then remove any excess paste with a sharp pair of scissors.

## BUDS

**5** Cut 28-gauge wire into thirds. Insert a wire into a small ball of white flowerpaste. Thin down the back of the bud to form a neck. Divide the bud into five sections using the plain-edge cutting wheel. Twist the petals very slightly.

## CALYX

**6** Roll five very small slender carrot-shaped pieces of pale holly/ivy flowerpaste. Flatten each and draw down a central vein using the fine end of the dresden veining tool. Pinch each sepal and add onto the back of the flowers and buds vein-side down.

## COLOURING

**7** Dust the flowers as desired – there are so many varieties that it is best to have a real flower or good photograph to use as a reference. I have used a mixture of plum and aubergine petal dusts for some of the flowers; plum, aubergine and coral for others and some I have dusted with a light mixture bluegrass, vine and white. The eye of the flower is generally paler and I mostly use white and daffodil petal dusts mixed together. Paint heavier markings around the base of the petals if desired using cyclamen liquid colour. Dust the calyx with a mixture of white and foliage green.

## LEAVES

**8** Roll out some pale holly/ivy flowerpaste, leaving a thick ridge for the wire. Cut out the leaf shape using either one of the two sizes of primrose leaf cutter. Insert a moistened 26-gauge wire into the ridge to support about half the length of the leaf.

**9** Soften the edges using the ball tool. Add an extra bumpy edge using the broad end of the dresden veining tool to pull out the edges of the leaf against the board. Vein using the hellebore leaf veiner. The smaller new leaves tend to be curled inwards.

**10** Dust with white, foliage and forest mixed together. Some auriculas have brighter foliage – I prefer the softer types. Catch the edge gently with aubergine. Spray lightly with edible spray varnish and tape the stems of the flowers and leaves together with quarter-width nile green floristry tape.

# ose

*Roses are the most popular celebration flowers used by florists and cake decorators. They create a wonderful focal point and also can be used successfully as secondary flowers in floral sprays and bridal bouquets. However, they often prove to be difficult for both the novice and experienced flower maker to produce consistently. There are many variations to making roses – the method described here is the one I use most.*

### Materials

*18-, 24-, 26-, 28- and 30-gauge white wires*
*Nile green floristry tape*
*White, pale vine green and holly/ivy flowerpaste*
*Fresh egg white*
*Vine green, edelweiss white, daffodil, sunflower, aubergine, plum, ruby, coral, forest green and foliage petal dusts*
*Cornflour*
*Half glaze or edible spray varnish (Fabilo)*

### Equipment

*Fine-nose pliers*
*Rolling pin*
*Rose petal cutters (TT549, 550, 551)*
*Foam pad*
*Metal ball tool (Cc)*
*Very large rose petal veiner (SKGI)*
*Dusting brushes*
*Cocktail stick, optional*
*Kitchen paper*
*Rose calyx cutter, optional*
*Sharp curved scissors*
*Set of three black rose leaf cutters (Jem)*
*Extra large rose leaf cutter (Jem)*
*Large briar rose leaf veiner (SKGI)*
*Smooth ceramic tool (HP)*

## ROSE CONE CENTRE

1 Tape over a half- to three-quarter length of 18-gauge white wire with half-width nile green floristry tape. Bend a large open hook in the end using fine-nose pliers. Form a ball of well-kneaded white flowerpaste into a cone shape to measure about two-thirds the length of the smallest rose petal cutter you are planning to use. Moisten the hook with fresh egg white and insert it into the rounded base of the cone. Push the hook into most of the length of the cone. Pinch the base of the paste onto the wire to secure the two together. Reshape the point of the cone if required – I tend to form a sharp point with a more rounded base. Allow to dry for as long as possible.

2 Colour a large amount of flowerpaste to the required colour; here I have used vine green petal dust to give a soft off-white base colour. I usually colour the paste paler than I want the finished rose to be – it is best to work against a lighter background so that the petal dusts will have a greater impact when applied.

## FIRST AND SECOND LAYERS

3 Roll out some of the coloured paste fairly thinly. Cut out four petals using the smaller of the two rose petal cutters you are planning to use. Place the petals on a foam pad and soften the edges using a metal ball tool – work half on the edge of the petal and half on the pad using a rolling action with the tool. Try not to frill

that you have enough of the petal to curl tightly to form a spiral effect around the cone. It is important that this cone is not visible from the overview of the finished rose. Do not worry about covering the cone near the base – there are plenty more petals to follow that will do that job. I tend to curl the petal in from the left-hand side. Leave the right-hand edge of the petal slightly open so that the next petal can be tucked underneath it.

**5** Moisten the remaining three petals and start the second layer by tucking a petal underneath the first petal on the cone. Stick down the edge of the first petal over the new petal. Place the next petal over the join created and then turn the rose to add the third petal. I tend to keep these petals open to start with so that I can get the positioning correct before tightening them around the cone to form a spiral shape. Leave one of the petals slightly open to take the first petal of the next layer. Some roses have slightly pinched petals – this can be done as you add each layer by pinching the top edge to create a slight point. This number of petals can be used to make small rosebuds but the cone base should be made slightly smaller so that the petals cover the whole of it.

## THIRD, FOURTH AND FIFTH LAYERS

**6** Roll out some more coloured flowerpaste and cut out nine petals using the same size cutter as earlier. Soften the edges and vein the petals as before. Cover the petals with a plastic bag

to stop them drying out – otherwise it is a case of cutting out and working on only three petals at a time. Tuck the first petal underneath the open petal from the previous layer of the rosebud and continue to add the other petals as described above, attaching them in layers of three petals at a time. It is important to keep positioning petals over joins in the previous layer and not to line up petals directly behind each other. Gradually start to loosen the petals slightly as you work on the fourth and fifth layers. Pinch and curl the edges slightly more as you attach the fifth layer.

## SIXTH LAYER

**7** Roll out more coloured flowerpaste and cut out three petals using the slightly larger rose petal cutter. Soften and vein as before. This time start to hollow out the centre of each petal using a large ball tool or by simply rubbing the petal with your thumb.

**8** Moisten the base of each petal creating a V shape. Attach to the rose as before, trying to place each petal over a join in the previous layer. Pinch either side of the petal at the base as you attach them so that it retains the cupped shape and allows the rose to breathe. Curl back the edges using a cocktail stick or just your fingers to create more movement in the petal edges. I tend to curl either edge of the petal, creating a more pointed petal shape. At this stage you have made what is termed a 'half rose'.

the edges at this stage as you are only taking away the raw cut edge of the petal. Vein each of the petals in turn using the double-sided rose petal veiner – dust with a little cornflour if needed to prevent sticking – especially if your veiner is being used for the first time. For smaller roses it is not always essential to vein the petals but the larger flowers benefit from it greatly.

**4** Place the first petal against the dried cone using a little fresh egg white to help stick it in place. It needs to be positioned quite high against the cone so

## FINAL LAYER

**9** I prefer to wire the petals individually for the final layer of the rose. This gives more movement and also a much stronger finished flower. Roll out some coloured flowerpaste, leaving a subtle ridge down the centre. Cut out the petal using the same size cutter as for the previous layer. Hook and moisten the end of a 26-gauge white wire. Insert it into the very base of the ridge. Soften the edges and vein as described previously. You will need cornflour dusting onto either the petal or the veiner at this stage to prevent them sticking together. Press the veiner firmly to create stronger veins. Remove from the veiner and hollow out the centre using your thumb and also start to curl back the edges. Allow the petal to dry slightly in a kitchen paper ring former. Repeat to make about eight to ten petals. The number varies with each rose that I make. As the petals are beginning to firm up you can keep going back to add extra curls to the edges if required.

## ASSEMBLY AND COLOURING

**10** I prefer to tape the individually wired petal around the half rose and then dust the rose as a whole – I find I balance the colour better this way. You might prefer to dust and then tape. It is best if the petals are not quite dry at this stage so that you can re-shape and

manipulate to form a more pleasing rose shape. Tape the first wired petal over a join in the petals of the half rose using half-width nile green tape. The next petal is placed onto the opposite side of the rose and then I continue adding the petals to cover gaps and joins in the previous layer. As before, remember not to place petals in line with petals of the layer underneath.

**11** Mix together edelweiss white, vine green, daffodil and sunflower petal dusts. Probe the flower with a brush loaded with this mix to add a 'glow' at the base of each petal on the back and front. I tend to be heavier with this colour on the back of the petals. Next, decide which colours you are using to colour the bulk of the rose. I have used a mixture of plum, coral and white for the rose pictured. Aim for the centre of the rose first of all to create a more intense focal point to the flower. Gradually tinge the edges of the surrounding and outer-wired petals.

## CALYX

**12** As the outer petals of the rose have been individually wired I find it is best to wire each sepal of the calyx, too. This gives a stronger finish but also allows the flower maker to represent a calyx with very long slender sepals. A quicker calyx may be added using a rose calyx cutter if

time or patience won't allow a wired calyx. Cut five lengths of 28-gauge white wire. Work a ball of holly/ivy coloured flowerpaste onto the wire creating a long tapered carrot shape. Place the shape against the board and flatten using the flat side of one of the double-sided veiners. If the shape looks distorted, simply trim into shape with a pair of sharp scissors.

**13** Place the flattened shape onto a foam pad or the palm of your hand and soften and hollow out the length using the metal ball tool. Pinch the sepal from the base to the tip. Cut fine 'hairs' into the edge of the sepal using a pair of sharp curved scissors. Repeat to make five sepals. I tend to leave one sepal without hairs – although remember there are some varieties of rose that have no hairs to their calyces at all.

**14** Dust each sepal on the outer surface with a mixture of foliage and forest green. Add tinges of aubergine mixed with plum or ruby petal dust. Use the same brush used for the green mixture and dust lightly on the inner surface of each sepal with white petal dust. Lightly glaze the back of each sepal with edible spray varnish.

**15** Tape the five sepals to the base of the rose, positioning a sepal over a join. Add a ball of paste for the ovary and pinch and squeeze it into a neat shape. Some florists' roses have almost no ovary – they have been bred out to prolong the life of the cut flower. Dust and glaze to match the sepals.

## LEAVES

**16** I don't often use rose leaves as a foliage in bridal bouquets, however, they are essential for arrangements. Rose leaves on commercial florists' roses tend to grow in sets of three or five. I generally make one large, two medium and two small

for each set. Roll out some holly/ivy flowerpaste, leaving a thick ridge for the wire – a grooved board can speed up this process considerably. Cut out the leaves using the rose leaf cutters. You will find that the black rose leaf set does not allow for very thick leaves – these tend to stick in the cutter. Insert a moistened 26-, 28- or 30-gauge white wire into the leaf depending on its size. I usually insert the wire about half way into the ridge.

**17** Soften the edge of the leaf and vein using the large briar rose leaf veiner. Pinch from behind the leaf to accentuate the central vein and give more movement to the leaf. Repeat to make leaves of various sizes. Tape over a little of each wire stem with quarter-width nile green floristry tape. Tape the leaves into sets of three or five, starting with the largest leaf and two medium-size leaves, one on either side. Finally add the two smaller leaves at the base.

**18** Dust the edges with aubergine and plum or ruby mixed together. Use this colour on the upper stems too. Dust the upper surface of the leaf in layers lightly with forest green and heavier with foliage and vine green. Dust the backs with white petal dust using the brush used for the greens. Spray with edible spray varnish.

Note the red roses on Everlasting Love (see pages 126–27) were made with a base of Christmas red and ruby mixed into the paste and then dusted with ruby, kiko and finally aubergine. The rose on the Coffee cake (see pages 116–17) was made with a pale vine green base and dusted with coral and plum mixed together and tinges of aubergine. The pink rose on pages 86–7 was dusted with plum petal dust.

# Fiddle-head fern

*I first came across these unfurled ferns in an American bridal magazine – they had been included in a bridal bouquet with arum lilies. They are so tightly furled that there is no need to add developing leaves. I loved the dark aubergine colouring, too – they look almost like curls of chocolate or liquorice that would be right at home in Willy Wonker's Chocolate factory!*

### Materials

*Pale holly/ivy flowerpaste*
*24- and 26-gauge white wire*
*Plum, aubergine and foliage green petal dusts*
*Edible spray varnish*

### Equipment

*Plain-edge cutting wheel (PME)*
*Fine-nose pliers*

**METHOD**

1 You will need to use full-length wires for this fern. Take a small ball of holly/ivy flowerpaste and wrap it around a 24- or 26-gauge (depending on the size of the fern) near to one end. Work the paste quickly and firmly up the wire to cover the length. You need to taper the thickness into a point at the tip.

2 Smooth the flowerpaste between your palms and also against a non-stick board using a rolling action. Mark a central vein down the length using the plain-edge cutting wheel. I sometimes dust the leaves at this stage and spray them and then start to curl them into the spiral, however, it might be better to curl and then dust as described below.

3 Hold the tip of the fern with fine-nose pliers and hold the other end of the wire with your other hand. Quickly and confidently curl the fern over and over to create a tight spiral shape. Release the pliers and then straighten up the length of the fern.

4 Dust in layers with plum, aubergine and tinges of foliage green. Spray with edible spray varnish.

# Croton foliage

*These decorative, glossy leaves are often known as*
*Codiaeum. This version is based on the variety*
*variegatum apple-leaf. They are very useful*
*additions to floral arrangements as they fill lots*
*of space and add extra detail to the overall design*

## LEAVES

**1**  These leaves are fairly fleshy allowing the flower-maker to use the flowerpaste slightly thicker than normal; the smaller leaves should be made slightly finer. Roll out some well-kneaded flowerpaste, leaving a fleshy central ridge for the wire – a grooved board may be used for this if desired. Cut out the leaf shape using one of the croton leaf cutters, or a sharp scalpel/plain-edge cutting wheel and one of the templates on page 141.

**2** Insert a moistened wire into the thick ridge of the leaf – the gauge will depend upon the size of the leaf. Try to insert the wire about halfway down the length of the leaf. Place the leaf on a foam pad and soften the edges with the large ball tool. Vein using the gardenia or mandevilla leaf veiner. Pinch the central vein of the leaf to emphasize it. Work the thick base of the leaf down onto the wire between your finger and thumb to create a fleshy stem covering. Allow to firm up a little before colouring.

## COLOURING

**3** Dust the leaves from the base fading out towards the edges with a mixture of plum, white and coral petal dusts mixed together. Mix together forest and foliage and dust the leaves from the edges towards the centre, blending the pink colouring and greens together slightly.

**4** Using the fine paintbrush, paint in the central and finer veins using a mixture of the green petal dusts and isopropyl alcohol/glaze cleaner. Use a toothbrush or stencil brush to flick specks of colour over the whole leaf – you might need rubber gloves for this job! Allow to dry. Dust lightly with aubergine and foliage if required to soften the painted detail. Spray lightly with edible spray varnish or dip into a half glaze.

### Materials

*White or pale melon-coloured flowerpaste*
*20-, 22-, 24-gauge white wires*
*Plum, white, coral, forest, foliage and*
  *aubergine petal dusts*
*Isopropyl alcohol/glaze cleaner*
*Edible spray varnish (Fabilo) (see page 11)*
  *or half glaze*

### Equipment

*Grooved board (optional)*
*Croton leaf cutters (AD), or see templates*
  *on page 141*
*Sharp scalpel or plain-edge cutting wheel (PME)*
*Foam pad*
*Large metal ball tool*
*Large gardenia or large mandevilla leaf veiner (SKGI)*
*Large flat dusting brushes*
*Fine paintbrush*
*Toothbrush or stencil brush*
*Rubber gloves*

# *I*ris

Iris is the Greek name for the messenger of
the goddess Hera. She brought messages from
Hera via the rainbow.
The iris family certainly does encompass all
the colours of the rainbow.

## STANDARD PETALS

1 Roll out some white flowerpaste leaving a thick ridge down the centre for the wire. Don't roll out the flowerpaste too thinly as the iris veiner is heavily veined and can cut through the paste if it is too thin. Cut out the petal shape using the narrow standard petal cutter (TT685) from the Dutch iris set.

2 Insert a moistened 26-gauge white wire into the thick ridge. Dust the petal lightly with the cornflour bag and place the petal carefully into the narrow standard petal veiner (TT685). Squeeze the two sides of the veiner together firmly. Remove the petal and using sharp scissors trim any excess flowerpaste that might have oozed from the sides of the veiner.

| Materials | Equipment |
|---|---|
| White and pale holly/ivy flowerpaste | Dutch iris cutters (TT683, 684, 685) |
| 18-, 24- and 26-gauge white wires | Cornflour bag (see page 10) |
| Daffodil, sunflower, bluebell, African violet, | Dutch iris veiners (SKGI) |
| deep purple, white and foliage petal dusts | Sharp scissors |
| Fresh egg white | Large tulip leaf veiner (SKGI) |
| Nile green floristry tape | Silk veining tool (HP) |
| Edible spray varnish | Plain-edge cutting wheel |

**3** Pinch the base of the petal and the tip and allow to dry slightly curved. Repeat to make three standard petals.

### FALL PETALS

**4** These are the larger base petals that protect the outer layer of the flower and are called tepals. Roll out some white flowerpaste, leaving a ridge and cut out the petal shape using the largest cutter (TT683) from the Dutch iris set. Insert a 24-gauge wire into the ridge. Soften the edges and vein using the largest veiner from the Dutch iris set.

**5** Remove the tepal from the veiner and frill the edges of the rounded section a little more using the silk veining tool – the Dutch iris veiner imprints a certain amount of frilling but this tends to look a little too 'solid'. Repeat to make three tepals. Dry in a curved position. Dust the central ridge with a mixture of daffodil and sunflower petal dusts.

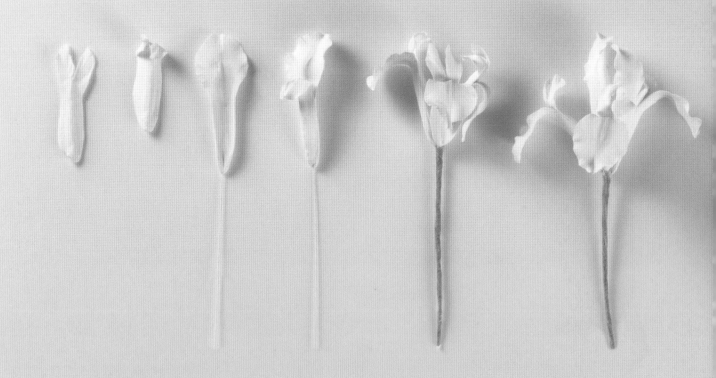

### CREST PETALS

**6** A single stamen is sandwiched in between the crest and the fall tepal, however, in the sugar version it is not essential to add this! Roll out some more white flowerpaste, again leaving a thick ridge. Crest petals need to be quite fleshy as the veining is particularly heavy with this section. These petals are not wired but need the extra support that the ridge can give. Cut out the shape using the crest petal cutter (684) from the Dutch iris set. Soften the edges and vein using the crest petal veiner. Remove from the veiner and add extra frilling to the two pointed sections at the top of the petal. Allow to firm up a little before attaching with a little fresh egg white to the top surface of the fall tepals. Flick back the two points of the crest petal. Allow to firm up further before assembling and colouring.

### ASSEMBLY AND COLOURING

**7** Tape together the three fall tepal/crest petal sections onto an 18-gauge wire with half-width nile green floristry tape.

**8** Next, thread the standard petals in between the fall sections and tape into position. Hopefully the flowerpaste is still pliable at this stage which will allow you to reshape the petals to create a more natural result.

**9** Dust a strong yellow streak to the underside of each fall tepal. Mix together bluebell, African violet and deep purple with a touch of white petal dust. Dust the whole flower, fading the colour towards the edges of each petal. Mix up a darker blend of the same colours – omitting white petal dust to add extra depth to the base of the petals and the backbone ridges of the crest petal. Steam to set the colour.

## BUD

**10** Form a ball of white flowerpaste into a cone shape. Insert a moistened 18-gauge wire into the broad end of the cone and then work the paste between your finger and thumb to create a longer neck.

**11** Divide the bud into three equal sections using the plain-edge cutting wheel. Pinch the bud back into a point. Dust as for the flower.

## FOR THE BRACTS

**12** These are in pairs down the stem. Roll out some pale holly/ivy flowerpaste and cut out freehand bract shapes using the plain-edge cutting wheel.

**13** Soften the edges and vein using the large tulip leaf veiner. Pinch a central vein down the bract. Add the bracts in pairs down the stem, staggering the height position slightly as you add each bract.

**14** Dust with foliage green petal dust. Spray lightly with edible spray varnish.

# Pavonia

*These unusual flowers are from South America. The bright pink, sometimes red, sepals create a wonderfully dramatic effect. The petals are smaller and generally a fairly dark purple – I have added a touch of artistic licence and made my version slightly cleaner in colour. I have also chosen not to use the leaves as they are large and tend to detract from the beauty of the flower. Further artistic licence could be used with the colouring of the flower – it would work well as a white flower for a wedding cake combined with white or soft-coloured roses.*

| Materials | Equipment |
|---|---|
| *White seed-head stamens* | *Scissors* |
| *Hi-tack non-toxic craft glue* | *Paintbrush* |
| *30-, 28- and 24-gauge white wires* | *Ceramic silk veining tool (HP)* |
| *Isopropyl alcohol* | *Stargazer B petal veiner (SKGI)* |
| *Plum, African violet and deep purple petal dusts* | |
| *White flowerpaste* | |
| *Nile green floristry tape* | |

**STAMENS**

1 Cut the tips off three stamens and cut them in half. Glue five of the six stamen threads together using a small amount of hi-tack glue. Flatten the base and attach to the end of a 24-gauge wire using a little more glue. Squeeze the stamens against the wire to secure them. Allow the glue to set. Slightly curl back the tips of the stamens. Paint with a mixture of alcohol and plum petal dust.

**2** Line up several small groups of seed-head stamens and glue each group together, starting at the centre and working up to the tips, and leaving a little of the length on either side unglued. Allow to dry and then cut each group in half. Trim the stamens to make them a little shorter and then glue them around the pistil, working down the wire slightly – rather like a spiral staircase effect. Allow to dry. Paint with a mixture of African violet and deep purple petal dusts and alcohol.

## PETALS

**3** Roll five small equal-sized balls of white flowerpaste. Form each ball into a teardrop shape and then flatten them against a non-stick board. Thin out and vein each petal using the ceramic silk veining tool to create fan shaped veining and petals.

**4** Moisten the base of the stamens and position each petal in turn to spiral tightly around the stamens. Dust with African violet and deep purple.

## SEPALS

**5** The number of outer sepals varies – I have used about ten to each flower. Cut lengths of 30- or 28-gauge wire into thirds. Work a small ball of white flowerpaste onto the wire and form a long tapered sepal shape. Flatten the sepal against the board using the flat side of the Stargazer B petal veiner. Next, place the sepal into the veiner to texture the surface.

**6** Pinch the petal from the base to the tip to create a central vein. Repeat to make the required number of sepals. As the paste starts to firm up a little you can start any reshaping and give the sepals a curve.

**7** Dust each sepal with plum petal dust, fading the colour slightly towards the tips of the sepals.

**8** Tape the sepals around the petals using half-width nile green floristry tape. It is good if the petals are still pliable at this stage, enabling you to create more interesting curves to the sepals.

## BUDS

**9** Insert a hooked moistened 24-gauge wire into the base of a cone shaped piece of white paste. Divide the surface into five petals. Twist slightly. Dust with African violet and deep purple. Add outer sepals as for the flower, making them slightly shorter and slimmer in shape.

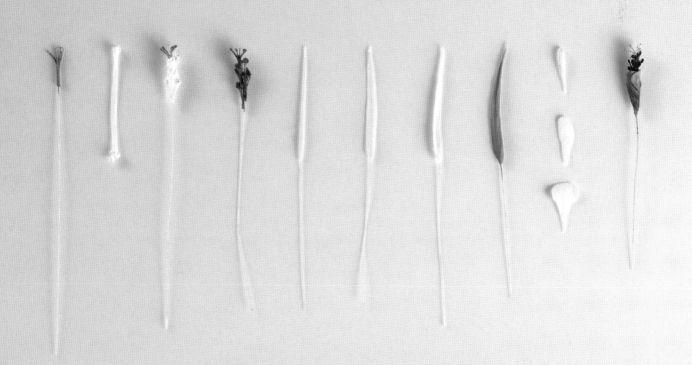

# Spathoglottis orchid

*There are over 40 species of Spathoglottis orchid distributed from southern India to southern China, Malaysia, the Philippines, Indonesia and New Caledonia.*

### COLUMN

**1** Cut a short length of 33-gauge wire. Roll a small ball of white flowerpaste and insert the wire into it. Work the paste down the wire leaving the tip slightly more rounded. Hollow the underside of the column by pressing it against the sides of the rounded end of the ceramic silk veining tool, hooking the rounded tip slightly over the top of the tool. Curve slightly. Add a tiny ball of flowerpaste onto the tip of the underside of the column to represent the anther cap. Divide into two sections using the sharp scalpel.

### LABELLUM/LIP

**2** Roll out a small piece of well-kneaded white flowerpaste, leaving a fine ridge for the wire. Cut out the lip shape using the odd-shaped Spathoglottis orchid cutter (824) – it always reminds me of a Diana Ross fishtail type dress! Insert a moistened 30-gauge wire into the ridge.

**3** Using the small ball tool soften and hollow out the two 'arms' of the shape. Pinch the length of the throat between your finger and thumb to create a slight ridge and make it look finer.

**4** Using the ceramic silk veining tool thin out and vein the tail shape using the veined end of the tool to create a more fan-shaped base. Pinch behind the 'arms' of the shape to push them forwards slightly. Bend the whole shape slightly to create a little more movement.

**5** Attach a tiny, almost heart-shaped piece of flowerpaste onto the lip. Divide the shape down the centre to create an indent. This is called the platform.

### LATERAL PETALS

**6** Roll out some white flowerpaste, leaving a ridge for the wire. Cut out the petal shape using the wider petal cutter (826). Insert a moistened 30-gauge wire into the ridge. Soften the edges with the ball tool.

**7** Vein in the cupped Christmas rose veiner. Pinch the petal slightly at the base and the tip to accentuate a central vein. Repeat to make two petals. Allow to dry curved backwards.

| Materials | Equipment |
|---|---|
| 28-, 30- and 33-gauge white wires | Scissors |
| White flowerpaste | Ceramic silk veining tool (HP) |
| White and nile green floristry tape | Sharp scalpel |
| Daffodil, sunflower, plum, African violet, white | Rolling pin |
| and vine green petal dusts | Spathoglottis orchid cutters (TT824–826) |
| | Small ball tool |
| | Cupped Christmas rose veiner (SKGI) |
| | Dresden/veining tool (J) |
| | Dusting brush |
| | Plain-edge cutting wheel (PME) |

## DORSAL AND LATERAL SEPALS

**8** These are made in the same way as the petals above, using the narrower of the two petal-shaped cutters. Curve the lateral sepals (legs) backwards and the dorsal (head) petal forwards.

## ASSEMBLY AND COLOURING

**9** Tape the curved column onto the lip/labellum using quarter-width white floristry tape. The column should curve towards the lip. Next add the two lateral petals onto either side of the throat and finally position the dorsal and lateral sepals slightly behind the arms to complete what almost looks like a figure (head, two arms and two legs).

**10** The back of the orchid has an elongated neck. Wrap a sausage of white flowerpaste around the back of the orchid and using your fingers and thumb work the paste together and down the wire to create a fine neck. Pinch off any excess paste. Blend the join between the neck and the petals using the broad end of the dresden tool – you might need a tiny amount of water to help the two dissolve and blend into each other. Curve the neck of the orchid slightly.

**11** Dust the raised heart-shaped platform in the throat with a mixture of daffodil and sunflower petal dusts. Mix together plum, African violet and white petal dusts to colour the whole orchid. Try to leave paler areas at the centre of each petal, increasing the colour on the edges. Add stronger colouring to the fishtail of the labellum. Use vine green at the base of the neck.

## BUDS

**12** Insert a 28-gauge wire into the base of a cone-shaped piece of white flowerpaste. Work the rounded base of the cone between your fingers and thumb to create an elongated neck shape. Smooth the neck between your palms and then curve it slightly. Create three sides to the top section of the bud by pressing it firmly between two fingers and a thumb.

**13** Mark a single line on each flattened side using the plain-edge cutting wheel. Repeat to make various sized buds. Dust as for the flower.

# Brassia orchid

*This spider-like orchid is from South America. It makes an interesting and useful addition*

*to any arrangement or bouquet as it looks light and airy and fills plenty of space, too.*

### COLUMN

**1** Attach a small ball of paste onto the end of a 28-gauge white wire. With your fingers, work the flowerpaste down the wire to form a teardrop shape. Place the shape against the rounded end of the ceramic silk veining tool to hollow out the underside. Curve the shape. Add an anther cap if desired by adding a tiny ball of flowerpaste onto the tip of the column.

Split the ball in half using a sharp scalpel. Paint the underside with cyclamen liquid spots.

### LABELLUM/LIP

**2** Roll out some well-kneaded flowerpaste leaving a thicker ridge at the centre for a wire. Cut out the lip shape using the Alstromeria petal cutter. Insert a moistened 26-gauge white wire into the ridge. Broaden the base of the petal to create a flap on either side using the broad end of the Dresden tool. Soften the edges of the petal and vein using the double-sided Stargazer B petal veiner.

**3** Frill the edges of the lip using the ceramic silk veining tool. Pinch back the base of the lip and pinch the tip into a

sharp point. There is a small raised platform at the base of the lip just in front of the column – this can be made quickly by pinching two ridges with fine tweezers or by adding an extra oval piece of paste divided into two sections with a scalpel. Allow to dry a little before colouring.

### OUTER PETALS

**4** There are five outer petals. When making orchids I tend to think of the petals as a figure – with one head, two arms and two legs. This orchid needs three long petals (head/legs) and two shorter petals (arms). Make each of these petals in exactly the same way, working a small ball of paste onto a length of 28-gauge white wire. Form the shape into a long pointed petal shape. Place against the work board and flatten the shape using the flat side of the Stargazer B veiner. Trim the edges if required using sharp scissors. Vein, using the Stargazer B petal veiner. Pinch the petal from the base to the tip to accentuate the central vein. Curve each petal back slightly.

54

| Materials | Equipment |
|---|---|
| *20-, 26- and 28-gauge white wires* | *Ceramic silk veining tool (HP)* |
| *White/cream flowerpaste* | *Sharp scalpel* |
| *Cyclamen liquid food colour* | *Fine paintbrush* |
| *Nile green floristry tape* | *Large Alstromeria petal cutter (TT910)* |
| *Vine green, edelweiss, aubergine, lemon, primrose,* | *Dresden veining tool (Jem)* |
| *foliage green and plum petal dusts* | *Stargazer B veiner (SKGI)* |
| | *Rubber veiner* |
| | *Sharp scissors* |
| | *Plain-edge cutting wheel* |
| | *Fine tweezers* |

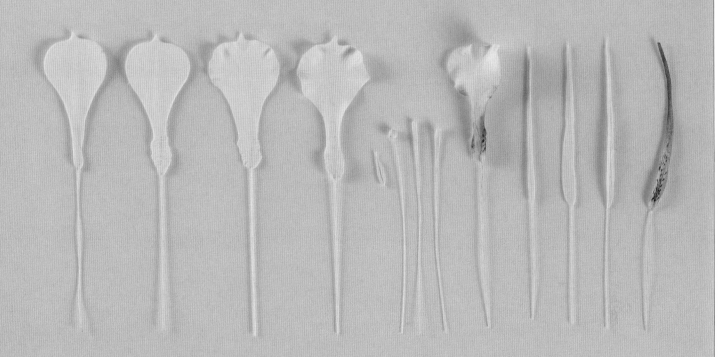

## COLOURING AND ASSEMBLY

5 Tape the column onto the labellum petal using half-width nile green floristry tape. Next add the two shorter outer petals (arms) and finally the outer three petals. If the flowerpaste is still pliable at this stage it will help to re-shape to create a more natural finish.

6 Dust the lip and outer petals lightly with a mixture of vine green and edelweiss petal dusts. Paint spots onto the lip and the outer petals using cyclamen liquid colour mixed with aubergine petal dust. Some Brassia orchids have raised

spots on the throat, others have simple spotted markings. Dust the edges of the orchid lightly with aubergine and plum if desired.

7 Add a platform onto the lip by adding a teardrop of paste split in half. This may be frilled slightly before using the broad end of the Dresden tool. Dust with a mixture of lemon/primrose.

## BUDS

8 These are long and slender. Add teardrop-shaped paste onto a 26-gauge white wire. Work into a slender

point. Divide into three using the plain-edge cutting wheel or sharp scalpel. Curve into shape.

## ASSEMBLY

9 Tape the buds onto a 20-gauge wire using half-width nile green floristry tape. Alternate the buds starting with the smallest and graduating the size as you work. Finally add the flowers. Dust the stem with foliage green petal dust. Add tinges of aubergine/plum to the tips and the base of the buds.

# Dillenia

*There are around sixty species of Dillenia distributed throughout South East Asia and as far as Fiji and northern Australia. The species illustrated here has white petals – but others have yellow petals with red or yellow stamens and there is also a species with white petals and dark red stamens. The flowers only last for a day followed by huge ripening fruits that are often eaten by elephants – hence it's other name of the elephant apple tree!*

## Materials

*White seed-head stamens*
*18-, 22-, 24-, 26- and 33-gauge white wires*
*White and mid holly/ivy flowerpaste*
*Nile green and brown floristry tape*
*Non-toxic hi-tack glue (Impex)*
*Vine green, white, sunflower, daffodil, aubergine, foliage green and forest petal dusts*
*Edible spray varnish (Fabilo)*

## Equipment

*Plain-edge cutting wheel (PME)*
*Sharp scissors*
*Dillenia petal cutter (AD),*
*or see template on page 141*
*Foam pad*
*Large metal ball tool*
*Large amaryllis veiner (ALDV)*
*Ceramic silk veining tool*
*Kitchen paper*
*Dillenia leaf cutters (AD)*
*Scalpel (optional)*
*Dresden veining tool (J)*
*Large pair of scissors*
*Large gardenia leaf veiner (SKGI)*
*Large gardenia leaf veiner (ALDV)*

## PISTIL

1 I prefer to make the pistil and first layer of stamens with cold porcelain (see pages 12–3) rather than sugar as this makes the stamens easier to attach later on. Cut ten short lengths of 33-gauge white wire. Roll a small ball of white flowerpaste, insert a wire and twiddle the paste down the wire to approximately 2.5 cm (1 in) in length. Smooth the shape between your palms and flatten slightly against a non-stick board. Draw down a central vein using the plain-edge cutting wheel. Repeat to make ten sections. Curve slightly.

2 Tape the ten sections together using half-width nile green floristry tape. Add a stronger 22-gauge wire to give extra support to the stamens, which are added next.

3 Wrap a ball of white flowerpaste just underneath the pistil and form it into an onion shape. Using the plain-edge cutting wheel or scalpel, draw a series of lines down the bulb shape to represent the inner, not-quite-formed stamens.

## STAMENS

4 Divide a bunch of white seed-head stamens into four groups. Line up the tips of the stamens in each group. Apply a little hi-tack glue at the centre of each group and blend the glue from the centre towards either end, leaving enough stamen length un-glued to give a realistic finish. Allow to set. Cut the stamens in half with sharp scissors.

5 Apply a little more glue to the base of the stamens and position each group in turn around the base of the pistil.

Squeeze the stamens against the bulb to secure them well. You might need to glue extra groups of stamens to fill in gaps – you will need to decide if this is the case as the number of stamens in each commercial bunch often varies! Allow to dry.

6 Dust the pistil, the filaments and the bulb shape lightly with a mixture of vine green and white petal dusts. Catch the tips with a light mixture of white, sunflower and daffodil petal dusts.

## PETALS

**7** Roll out some well-kneaded white flowerpaste leaving a central ridge for the wire. Cut out a petal shape using the dillenia petal cutter and insert a hooked moistened 26-gauge white wire into the base of the thick ridge.

**8** Place the petal onto a foam pad and soften the edges using the large ball tool. Vein the petal using the large amaryllis petal veiner.

**9** Next, frill the top edge of the petal using the ceramic silk veining tool – this can be done against the non-stick board or by placing the petal over your index finger and frilling against your finger. Use short bursts of rolling rather than swooping using the ceramic silk veining tool over the surface. Hollow out the centre of the petal slightly using your thumb, then leave dry cupped in a kitchen paper ring (see page 9). Repeat to make five petals.

## DUSTING AND ASSEMBLY

**10** Dust the base of each petal on both the back and the front lightly with a mixture of vine green and white petal dusts.

**11** Tape the five petals around the stamens centre using half-width nile green floristry tape.

## CALYX

**12** The calyx is fairly fleshy. Insert a 26-gauge wire into a ball of mid holly/ivy flowerpaste. Work the paste at the base to form a cone shape. Flatten the paste and place in the palm of your hand to thin the edges and hollow the centre with the metal ball tool. Pinch the base and the rounded edge to shape the sepal. Repeat to make five sepals.

**13** Dust with vine green petal dust and tape onto the back of the flower using half-width nile green floristry tape, positioning each sepal in between the join in the petals.

## BUDS

**14** Bend a large hook in the end of a half-length 22-gauge wire. Roll a ball of mid holly/ivy flowerpaste and insert the moistened hook into the base. Neaten the join between the bud and the wire which will help to secure the two together. Using the plain-edge cutting wheel divide the surface into five sections to represent the five sepals of the calyx. Allow to dry and then thicken the stem slightly with a few layers of half-width nile green tape.

**15** Dust the top of the bud with aubergine petal dust. Colour the rest of the bud with foliage and vine green, blending the colours together as you apply them. Spray lightly with edible spray varnish.

## LEAVES

**16** The leaves of the tree are huge, however, they tend to appear towards the end of the flowering season, just like the magnolia tree. I have scaled down the size of the leaves somewhat. Roll out some mid holly/ivy flowerpaste, leaving a thick ridge for the wire. Cut out the leaf shape using either one of the dillenia leaf cutters or freehand, using a sharp scalpel or plain-edge cutting wheel.

**17** Insert a 26- or 24-gauge wire into about half the length of the leaf. Soften the edges of the leaf with the ball tool. Next, create a serrated edge by pulling out the paste from the edge of the leaf against the board using the broad end of the dresden veining tool. Vein using the large gardenia leaf veiner. Pinch the leaf from the base to the tip to accentuate the central vein. Allow to firm up a little before dusting.

**18** Dust the edges and the base of the leaf with aubergine petal dust. Use layers of forest, foliage and plenty of vine petal dusts to colour the main body of the leaf, fading the colour towards the edges. Allow to dry, then glaze lightly with edible spray varnish.

**19** Tape the buds and leaves onto a couple of 18-gauge wires with brown floristry tape. Thicken the stem as you work by adding strips of kitchen paper. Create a gnarled effect to the branch by wrapping lengths of twisted brown floristry tape around the areas where the buds, flowers and leaves appear from the branch. Polish the branch using the side of a large pair of scissors.

# Michelia

*There are around forty-five species of michelia. The tree is sometimes known as the banana shrub because of the heavy sweet scent of the flowers. They are closely related to the magnolia family although tend to be more tropical-loving in habitat.*

### Materials

*22-, 24-, 26- and 33-gauge wire*
*Pale holly/ivy and pale yellow flowerpaste*
*Vine green, sunflower, aubergine, daffodil, tangerine, coral, foliage and forest petal dusts*
*Nile green floristry tape*
*Edible spray varnish (Fabilo)*

### Equipment

*Sharp curved scissors*
*Plain-edge cutting wheel*
*Michelia petal cutters (AD)*
*Foam pad*
*Stargazer B petal veiner (SKGI)*
*Kitchen paper*
*Dillenia leaf cutters (AD)*
*Mandevilla leaf veiner (SKGI)*
*Large dusting brush*

## PISTIL AND STAMENS

**1** Insert a moistened 22-gauge wire into a ball of pale holly/ivy flowerpaste. Work the paste down the wire to create a pistil length of about 2.5 cm (1 in) – although this does vary between species.

**2** Hold the pistil upside down and using a pair of curved scissors snip into the surface to create fine hairs. Curl back some of the lower hairs and squeeze those that are towards the tip of the pistil in tighter. Dust with vine green petal dust.

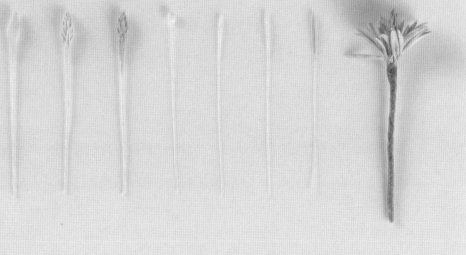

**3** Cut short lengths of 33-gauge wire. Attach a very small ball of pale yellow flowerpaste to the end of the wire and work it down the wire to form the anther of the stamen. Mark a line down the length using the plain-edge cutting wheel. Repeat to make about twenty stamens. Tape these around the pistil with nile green floristry tape. You might need to make some more stamens at this stage – it is very much a personal thing. Dust them with sunflower and a light dusting of aubergine. Allow to dry and then steam (see page 11) to set the colour.

### PETALS

**4** You need to make ten petals for the flower – I use two cutter sizes that are fairly close in size. Roll out some pale yellow flowerpaste leaving a thick ridge for the wire. The petals of this flower are fairly fleshy so do not roll the paste too fine. Cut out a petal shape using the michelia petal cutter.

**5** Place the petal on a foam pad and soften the edge. Vein using the Stargazer B veiner. Hollow out the centre of the petal slightly and dry in a slightly cupped shape using a kitchen paper ring former (see page 9). Repeat to make five large and five slightly smaller petals.

## COLOURING AND ASSEMBLY

6 Dust each petal with a mixture of sunflower and daffodil. Try to leave some of the pale yellow base colour shining through. Use the dust from the base of each petal on the back and the front, fading the colour towards the tip, then bring in some colour from the edges. Mix together tangerine and coral petal dusts to add tinges to the edges of the petals.

7 Tape the smaller five petals around the stamens using half-width nile green floristry tape. Add the larger petals slightly behind and in between the small petals. If the paste is still pliable at this stage it will be a bonus to help you reshape the flower to create more movement. Allow to dry and then steam to set the colour and give a slightly waxy finish.

## LEAVES

8 These are big and great for filling space in a floral design. Roll out some pale holly/ivy flowerpaste, leaving a thick ridge for the wire. Cut out the leaf shape using one of the several sizes of dillenia leaf cutters or freehand with the plain-edge cutting wheel. Insert a 26-, 24- or 22-gauge wire, depending on the size of the leaf. Soften the edge and vein using the large mandevilla leaf veiner. Pinch the leaf at the base and at the tip to accentuate the central vein. Allow to firm up before dusting.

9 Dust in layers with a large brush. Use foliage and forest green to create depth, using the side of the brush to drag against the raised areas of the leaf pattern. Overdust with vine green. Spray lightly with edible spray varnish.

# Magnolia

*Magnolias are considered to be one of the oldest plants in the world. Their flowers can vary in size, shape and colouring. They are very elegant, graceful flowers to use on cakes.*

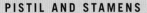

### PISTIL AND STAMENS

**1** The pistil and stamens are made in the same way as the centre for the michelia (see pages 60–1). Curve the stamens a little more than in the michelia. Dust the pistil with vine green and then add tinges of aubergine. The stamen colour varies from cream to yellow through to plum or aubergine. I like to make very dark centres so tend to dust them heavily with aubergine petal dust. Spray the centre lightly with edible spray varnish and allow to dry – this should prevent the aubergine dust dropping onto the white magnolia petals later.

### PETALS

**2** Roll out some white flowerpaste leaving a central ridge. Cut out a petal using the largest magnolia petal cutter. Insert a moistened 26-gauge wire into the thick ridge. Soften the edge and vein using the Stargazer B veiner.

**3** Hollow out the top section of the petal using a large ball tool or your thumb. Curl back the outer edges of petal. Dry in a kitchen paper ring former (see page 9). Repeat to make three.

**4** Repeat Step 2 for the medium and small petals, making three of each size. Cup and pinch the medium petals slightly towards the tip. Pinch the smaller petals from the base to the tip to curl them back. Allow to firm up before dusting.

**5** Dust a light streak down the back of each petal using plum and white petal dusts mixed together. Add stronger plum colouring if desired and then a little aubergine dust towards the base.

**6** Tape the three medium petals around the stamens using half-width nile green floristry tape. Next, add the three large petals slightly behind and in between the previous three. Finally add the three smaller curved petals to complete the flower.

**7** Open buds can be made effectively by taping three medium and three small petals around a tapered bud shape wired onto a 22-gauge wire. Dust as for the flower.

### LEAVES

**8** Follow the instructions for the michelia foliage (see page 62) using the large or extra large gardenia leaf veiner to texture the leaves. Use layers of forest, foliage and vine green to dust them but make sure they are not as dark as the Michelia leaves. Glaze lightly with spray varnish.

| Materials | Equipment |
|---|---|
| *22-, 24- and 26-gauge white wires* | *Sharp curved scissors* |
| *White and holly/ivy flowerpaste* | *Magnolia petal cutters (TT452, 453, 454)* |
| *Plum, white, aubergine, forest, foliage and* | *Stargazer B petal veiner (SKGI)* |
| *vine green petal dusts* | *Large gardenia leaf veiner (SKGI)* |
| *Nile green floristry tape* | *Extra large gardenia leaf veiner (ALDV)* |
| *Edible spray varnish (Fabilo)* | |

# Snake vine

## Materials

Cold porcelain (see pages 12–3)
22-, 26-, 28-, 30- and 33-gauge white wire
Pale yellow and pale holly/ivy flowerpaste
White seed-head stamens
Nile green floristry tape
Vine green, ruby, sunflower, daffodil, foliage, forest,
aubergine, and white petal dusts
Hi-tack non-toxic craft glue (Impex)
Edible spray varnish (Fabilo)

## Equipment

Dusting brush
Fine tweezers
Grooved board
Rolling pin
Australian rose petal cutter (TT349)
Fine curved scissors
Metal ball tool
Cupped Christmas rose leaf veiner (SKGI)
Ceramic silk veining tool (HP)
Non-stick board
Plain-edge cutting wheel (PME)
Hellebore leaf veiner (ALDVAL)

*The Snake vine from Australia belongs to the same family that includes the Dillenia (see pages 56–9). The plant is an evergreen scrambler growing to lengths of 1.2 m (4 ft) or more. Although the flowers of the plant are quite stunning in golden yellow, white, cream or orange they tend to have a fairly unpleasant scent.*

## PISTIL

1 I usually make this section of the flower with cold porcelain – this allows for easier construction of the stamen centre. Cut ten short lengths of 33-gauge wire. Work a tiny ball of cold porcelain onto the end of each wire, forming the shape into a slender teardrop. Slightly flatten each teardrop and curl back the tips. Tape the ten sections together using quarter-width nile green floristry tape. Dust with vine green. Add tinges of ruby to the tips of the pistil if desired.

**3** Dust the length of the stamens with vine green petal dust and the tips/anthers with sunflower and daffodil.

## PETALS

**4** Roll out some pale yellow flowerpaste leaving a thick ridge for the wire – a grooved board will speed up this process a little. Cut out the petal shape using the Australian rose petal cutter. Insert a short length of moistened 28-gauge white wire into the base of the ridge.

## COLOURING AND ASSEMBLY

**7** Dust the base of each petal with vine green petal dust. Mix together daffodil and sunflower to dust the whole of each petal from the edges to the base.

**8** Tape the five petals around the stamens using quarter-width nile green tape. Allow to flower to dry and then steam lightly to set the dust and give a more waxy finish.

## STAMENS

**2** Form several small groups of seed-head stamens and glue each group from the centre with hi-tack craft glue. Work from the centre of the stamens towards the tips on either end, leaving a little of the stamen length unglued. Try not to use too much glue as this will slow down the drying process. Allow the glue to dry and then cut each group in half. Trim off most of the excess glue from each. Attach using a little extra glue onto the base of the pistil to create an attractive ring of stamens. Pinch them at the base to secure them. Allow to dry, then using fine tweezers, 'open-up' the stamens slightly.

**5** Cut the petal shape using curved scissors to create a more heart-shaped petal. Soften the edges using the metal ball tool and then place into the cupped Christmas rose leaf veiner to texture the petal.

**6** Create a tight frilled edge to the petal using the ceramic silk veining tool. Cup the centre of the petal on either side of the wire using the small end of the metal ball tool. Curl the petal edges back slightly. Repeat to make five.

## CALYX

**9** I prefer to wire each of the sepals of the calyx to give them more movement and strength. Cut five short lengths of 33-gauge wire. Insert a wire into the base of a small teardrop-shaped piece of pale holly/ivy flowerpaste. Place the teardrop against the non-stick board and flatten it using the flat side of a rubber leaf/petal veiner. Trim the edge of the shape if needed and then hollow out the length using a small ball tool. Pinch the sepal from the base to the tip to create a central vein. Repeat to make five.

**10** Dust with vine green and foliage petal dusts. Add tinges of ruby to the edges. Tape onto the back of the flower using quarter-width nile green floristry tape, positioning each sepal in between two petals.

## BUDS

**11** Bend a hook in the end of a 26-gauge wire. Form a teardrop-shaped piece of pale yellow flowerpaste. Moisten the hook and insert it into the base of the teardrop. Divide the bud into five petals using the plain-edge cutting wheel. Colour and add a calyx as described for the flower but this time close the sepals tightly around the bud.

## LEAVES

**12** I tend to wire the smaller leaves onto 33- and 30-gauge wires using the technique described for the calyx. Vein each leaf using the top section of the hellebore leaf veiner where you will find the veins are more suitable for this size of leaf being tighter together. For the larger leaves roll out the pale holly/ivy flowerpaste leaving a thick ridge. Cut out the leaf using the plain-edge cutting wheel. Insert a 28- or 26-gauge wire into the leaf, depending on its size.

**13** Soften the edge of the leaf and vein using the hellebore leaf veiner again. Pinch the length to accentuate the central vein. Curve the leaves back slightly. Repeat to make the required number.

**14** Dust in layers of forest, foliage and vine green. Add tinges to the leaf edges using a mixture of ruby and aubergine petal dusts. Dust the back of each leaf with white petal dust. Spray lightly with edible spray varnish.

**15** Tape the leaves in pairs or sets of three onto a 22-gauge wire using nile green floristry tape. Gradually increase the size of the leaves and add the odd bud where the leaves appear from the main stem. Continue to add more leaf groups and flowers to create a long trailing stem. Dust the upper surface of the stem with ruby and aubergine petal dusts mixed together.

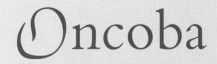

# Oncoba

*The fragrant white flowers of this African spiny shrub make great focal flowers to use on cakes. The fruit gives the plant its more common name of the snuffbox tree as the dried fruit has often been used to make both snuffboxes and tribal ankle rattles in the past! I used a botanical illustration of this flower as my inspiration – adding a touch of artistic licence en route.*

## Materials

White and holly/ivy green flowerpaste

22-, 24-, 28-, 26- and 33-gauge white wires

White seed-head stamens

Daffodil, sunflower, edelweiss, vine green, foliage, forest, lilac, lichen glow, dessert storm and aubergine petal dusts

African violet and deep purple craft dusts

Isopropyl alcohol/glaze cleaner

Non-toxic hi-tack craft glue

Nile green floristry tape

Edible spray varnish (Fabilo)

Styrofoam balls

## Equipment

Ceramic tool

Plain-edge tweezers

Fine paintbrush

Christmas rose cutter (TT282)

Cupped Christmas rose cutter or Stargazer B petal veiner (SKGI)

Silk veining tool and smooth frilling tool (HP)

Ball tool

Flat bristled dusting brush

Dresden tool

Plain-edge cutting wheel

Sage leaf cutters (TT852, 855)

Large gardenia leaf veiner (SKGI)

Sharp scalpel or scissors

Christmas rose cutter (TT282)

Calyx cutter (T526)

## PISTIL

1 Roll a small ball of very pale green flowerpaste made from a mixture of white and holly/ivy flowerpaste. Insert a 24-gauge wire. Work the paste down the wire between your finger and thumb leaving the tip more bulbous. Thin down the length and flatten the top. Using the rounded end of the ceramic tool, indent the centre of the flattened end. Next, pinch a series of fine ridges around the edges using a pair of plain-edge tweezers. Add a ball of pale green flowerpaste to the base of the pistil to represent the ovary. Pinch it against the wired section to secure it in place. Leave to dry.

2 Dust lightly with a mixture of edelweiss and vine green. Darken the ovary with full strength vine green and foliage petal dusts. Dilute some African violet and deep purple craft dusts with isopropyl alcohol and paint each of the ridges an intense purple.

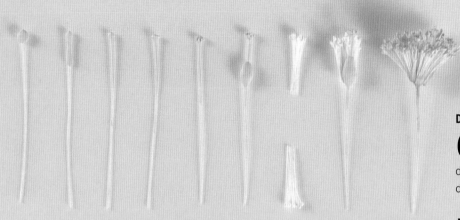

## DUSTING AND ASSEMBLY

**6** Dust the base of each petal lightly using edelweiss and vine green petal dusts – I prefer to use a flat bristled dusting brush.

**7** Tape the petals around the stamen centre using half-width nile green floristry tape. Create a ring of petals and then add a second layer, positioning the petals to cover a join in the first layer.

## STAMENS

**3** Divide a whole bunch of seed-head stamens into four or five groups. Line up the tips and glue them together from the centre using hi-tack glue, leaving enough of the stamens unglued at either end to give them movement. Squeeze the glue into the stamens to create a strong bond and flatten them, too. Allow to dry. Using sharp scissors, cut the stamens in half and trim off any excess length from the base of each. Attach around the base of the ovary using a little softened flowerpaste or fresh egg white mixture. Allow to dry. Dust the length of the stamens with a soft mixture of vine green and edelweiss petal dusts. Dust the tips with a mixture of sunflower and daffodil yellow.

## PETALS

**4** The number of petals can vary between varieties – the floral illustration I copied had about twenty petals. Other photographs I found of the flower only had about ten. I have squashed the Christmas rose cutter (TT282) to produce a more slender petal shape. Roll out some white flowerpaste leaving a thick ridge for the wire (a grooved board may also be used for this job). Cut out a petal shape using the Christmas rose cutter. Hold the petal firmly between your finger and thumb and insert a moistened 28-gauge white wire into the thick ridge of the petal – about a third of the length. Soften the edges of the petal and then vein using either the cupped Christmas rose veiner or the Stargazer B veiner.

**5** Place the petal over your index finger and frill the edges using the silk veining tool at intervals around the edge of the petal. Cup the petal slightly using the ball tool and then allow to firm up a little before adding to the flower. Repeat to make between ten but no more than twenty petals.

## CALYX

**8** Roll out a small amount of green flowerpaste leaving a raised bump in the centre. Cut out the shape using the calyx cutter. Soften the edges of each sepal using the ball tool. Hollow out the length using the broad end of the Dresden tool. Thread and secure onto the back of the flower using fresh egg white. Dust lightly with vine green and holly/ivy. Steam the flower to set the colour.

## LEAVES

**9** Roll out some green flowerpaste, leaving a thick ridge. The leaves can be slightly on the fleshy side. Cut out a basic leaf shape using the plain-edge cutting wheel or a sage leaf cutter. Insert a moistened 26- or 24-gauge wire, depending on the size of the leaf. Soften the edge and vein using the large gardenia leaf veiner. Create a serrated edge to the leaf using either a sharp scalpel or scissors to cut and flick into the edge. Pinch the leaf from the base to the tip to accentuate the central vein. Allow to firm up a little before dusting.

**10** Dust in layers with forest, foliage and vine green. Add a tinge of lilac to the edge. Spray lightly with edible spray varnish. Tape over the wire using half-width nile green floristry tape.

## FRUIT

**11** Bend a hook in the end of a 22-gauge wire. Apply a little non-toxic glue and thread it through a styrofoam ball. Pull the wire deep to secure the hooked end into the ball. Allow to dry overnight.

**12** Roll out some pale green flowerpaste fairly thickly. Apply a little fresh egg white to the ball and cover it with the paste. Fold the paste around the ball to create four corners. Pinch together and then remove the excess using a pair of sharp curved scissors. Smooth over the joins using a small rolling pin and then your fingers.

**13** Create a series of lines down the fruit using the side of the ceramic tool. Add a calyx as for the flower – but this time flick the sepals back from the fruit.

**14** Model a tiny dried version of the pistil from the flower onto a 33-gauge wire. Cut the wire very short and insert into the fruit. Allow to dry a little before dusting.

**15** Dust in layers with lichen glow, dessert storm, and foliage and lightly with aubergine. Finally, spray lightly with edible spray varnish.

# Milkweed

*The genus is named after the ancient god of the art of healing, Asklepios.*

*The hybrid form I have copied was bought as a cut flower from a florist.*

*Asclepia/milkweed was first cultivated in England in 1669 although*

*it actually originates from North America.*

### CENTRE

**1** Bend a hook in the end of 26-gauge wire. Attach a ball of cream flowerpaste over the hook. Flatten the top and then hollow out the top using the rounded end of the ceramic tool. Allow to dry. Dust with vine green and a little sunflower.

**2** Form five equal size cone shaped pieces of cream flowerpaste. Open up the base section of each cone using the pointed end of the ceramic tool. Snip the tip into two sections and then pinch each to thin them and curl them back.

| Materials | Equipment |
|---|---|
| *26- and 33-gauge white wire* | *Smooth ceramic tool (HP)* |
| *Cream and holly/ivy flowerpaste* | *Dusting brush* |
| *Vine green, sunflower, tangerine, ruby,* | *Sharp scissors* |
| *vine green and foliage petal dusts* | *Dresden tool* |
| *Fresh egg white* | *Non-stick board* |
| *Nile green floristry tape* | *Stargazer B petal veiner* |
| | *Small ball tool* |
| | *Plain-edge cutting wheel* |

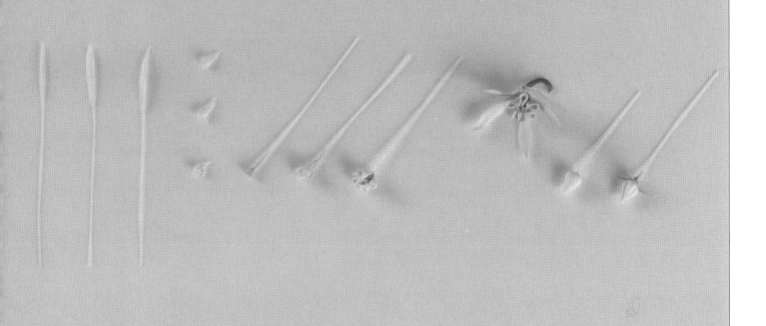

3 Make up a sticky glue using flowerpaste and fresh egg white blended together with the broad end of the Dresden tool to form a very stretchy sticky sugar glue. Attach each of the five hollowed cone shapes around the dried wired centre to make up the first layer of the flower. Allow to dry. Dust with tangerine and ruby petal dusts.

## PETALS

4 Cut five short lengths of 33-gauge white wire. Form a cone of cream flowerpaste and insert a wire into it. Blend and work the paste down the wire to form a cigar shape. Place against the non-stick board and flatten using the flat side of the stargazer B petal veiner. Soften the edges and vein using the two textured sides of the same veiner. Repeat to make five.

5 Hollow out the length of the back of each petal using the small ball tool. Pinch and shape each petal to create a little movement. Dust using tangerine and then edge with ruby.

6 Tape the five petals onto the back of the wired centre using half-width nile green floristry tape.

## CALYX

7 Roll five fine pieces of holly/ivy coloured flowerpaste. Flatten, pinch and attach onto the back of the flower so that each sepal is visible between the petals.

## BUDS

8 Bend a hook in the end of a 26-gauge wire. Insert into a small chubby cone shaped piece of fowerpaste. Divide into five sections using the plain-edge cutting wheel. Indent the length of each section using the smooth ceramic tool. Add a calyx as for the flower. Dust the buds with tangerine and ruby – aiming the colour at the edge of each marked petal. Dust the calyces with vine and foliage green mixed together.

# Cymbidium orchid

*Cymbidium orchids are a very popular bridal flower, adding an instant exotic feel to any bridal bouquet. The size and colour variations of the hybrid cymbidium orchids allow the flower maker to use artistic licence easily.*

## COLUMN

1 Take the column mould from the cymbidium orchid veiner set. Dust it lightly with cornflour. Form a ball of well-kneaded cream flowerpaste into a long cone shape and press into the mould. Use the other side of the mould to squeeze and press the paste to form a defined shape. Remove the shape from the mould and carefully neaten the edges with a fine pair of scissors. Insert a moistened 22-gauge wire into the thick base of the column. Curve and allow to dry.

| Materials | Equipment |
|---|---|
| Cream flowerpaste | Cymbidium orchid veiner set (ALDV) |
| 22- and 24-gauge white wires | Cornflour bag (see page 10) |
| Plum, aubergine, sunflower, daffodil | Fine scissors |
| and white petal dusts | Dusting brush |
| Cyclamen liquid food colour | Fine paintbrush |
| Fresh egg white | Cymbidium orchid cutters |
| | Ceramic silk veining tool (HP) |
| | Ball tool |

2 Dust the back of the column with a mixture of plum and aubergine petal dusts. Try to keep the tip (anther cap) of the column cream. Dust this with a light mixture of sunflower, daffodil and white. Paint lots of fine spots onto the underside of the column using a fine paintbrush and cyclamen liquid food colour.

### THROAT (LABELLUM)

3 Roll out some cream flowerpaste leaving a thicker raised area at the centre. Cut out the throat shape using the throat cutter from the cymbidium orchid cutter set. Dust the throat mould with cornflower and carefully position the cut out throat into the throat mould/veiner. Press firmly to form the shape and allow the raised section of the paste to fill the central platform area of the throat veiner/mould. Remove the shape from the mould.

4 Frill the edges of the bottom section of the throat using the silk veining tool. Attach onto the column using fresh egg white. Curl the top edges of the throat petal back slightly. Allow to dry a little before colouring.

5 Dust the raised platform at the heart of the throat with a mixture of daffodil and sunflower petal dusts. Paint heavy markings onto the throat using a fine paintbrush and cyclamen liquid colour. It is best to have a real flower or a good photograph at this stage to copy and help create realistic markings.

## LATERAL PETALS

6 Roll out some more cream flowerpaste leaving a thick ridge for the wire. Cymbidium orchids are quite fleshy so the paste can be rolled a little thicker than usual. Cut out the petal using the lateral petal cutter from the cymbidium orchid set. Insert a moistened 24-gauge white wire into the thick ridge. Soften the edges using a ball tool. Vein, using the lateral petal veiner from the cymbidium veiner set. Repeat to make a second petal turning the cutter over to create a mirror image. I think of these as arms. Curve the petals and allow to firm up a little before dusting.

## DORSAL AND LATERAL SEPALS

7 These are made in the same way as described above for the petals. You will need to make one dorsal and two lateral sepals. I tend to think of these as the flower's head and legs.

8 The petals and sepals can be dusted before or after assembling the flower. I have used a mixture of aubergine and plum to dust each from the base fading out towards the edges and then dust in from the edges to create a more balanced finish.

9 Tape the lateral petals (arms) onto either side of the throat using half-width nile green floristry tape. Next add the dorsal sepal behind the arms and finally the lateral sepals (legs) at the base. If the paste is still slightly pliable at this stage it will help you to reshape the flower slightly to create a more realistic finish. Allow the flower to dry and then hold over a jet of steam to help set the colours and leave a slight waxy effect to the finished flower.

# Lotus

*Often known as the Sacred Lotus (Nelumbo), this makes a wonderful majestic*

*space filler for any cake or flower arrangement. Even the foliage can be useful when*

*folded into fan shapes to add interest in arrangements with other flowers.*

## POD

**1** I prefer to use cold porcelain (see pages 12–3) for the pod so that I can attach the stamens easily and neatly onto the pod using non-toxic craft glue. Using fine-nose pliers, bend a large hook in the end of an 18-gauge wire. Knead some pale green cold porcelain until smooth. Form a ball shape into a cone and insert the moistened hooked wire into the fine end of the shape – work the paste onto the wire to secure it firmly. Flatten the broad end and pinch the edges to form the pod shape.

**2** Pinch a series of ridges around the sides of the pod using a pair of plain-edge angled tweezers. Pinch slightly around the circumference of the pod too.

**3** Create holes into the top of the pod using the pointed end of the smooth ceramic tool. Next, roll some small balls/seeds of green cold porcelain to sit into each of the holes on the pod. Open up the centre of some of the seeds using the needle tool or strong wire. Dust the surface of the pod as desired – the colour varies a little between varieties – it can be yellow, bright green or a darker green with aubergine tinges.

### Materials
*Small amount of cold porcelain (optional)*
*Hi-tack non-toxic craft glue (Impex)*
*18-, 20-, 22- and 26-gauge white wires*
*White and green flowerpaste*
*Sunflower, daffodil, dessert storm, edelweiss, vine green, plum, African violet, foliage, lilac, aubergine and forest petal dusts*
*Seed-head stamens*
*Nile green floristry tape*
*Fresh egg white*

### Equipment
*Fine-nose pliers*
*Plain-edge angled tweezers*
*Smooth ceramic tool (HP)*
*Needle tool (PME) or strong wire*
*Sage leaf cutters (TT852, 855)*
*Large metal ball tool (Cc)*
*Stargazer B petal veiner (SKGI)*
*Scissors*
*Plain-edge cutting wheel*
*Diamond Jubilee rose cutters (TT776, 777)*
*Very large nasturtium leaf veiner (SKGI)*
*Edible spray varnish (Fabilo)*

## STAMENS

4 You will need about two bunches of seed-head stamens to create a full centre. Make several smaller bunches of stamens glued at the centre to secure each bundle together. Flatten the glue into the stamen threads, leaving enough length unglued to create an attractive centre. Leave to dry slightly, then cut each group in half using scissors. Trim as required and attach using a little more hi-tack glue onto the sides of the pod. Allow to dry. Using tweezers open up and give the stamens a little movement. Dust with sunflower, daffodil and dessert storm.

## PETALS

5 Roll out some white flowerpaste, leaving a thick ridge for the wire. Cut out the petal shape using the largest of the sage leaf cutters. Insert a moistened 26-gauge white wire into the base of the ridge.

6 Soften the cut edge of the petal using the large metal ball tool – work half on the edge of the paste and half on your hand or foam pad using a rolling action. Vein the petal using the Stargazer B veiner or similar. Hollow out the centre of the petal using either the large ball tool or by rubbing it carefully with your thumb.

7 Cut a sheet of kitchen paper diagonally in half. Twist it onto itself and then tie it into a ring to make a former to rest the petal into the required cupped shape to dry. This allows the petal to breathe and dry faster than using a 'set' former. Repeat to make several petals – the number varies between varieties. I often add a few smaller petals, too, using the same method.

## DUSTING AND ASSEMBLY

8 Dust the base of each petal using a light mixture of edelweiss and vine green petal dusts. Heavily dust the main body of each petal using plum petal dust. Tinge the edges with African violet.

9 Tape the petals tightly around the stamen/pod centre using full- or half-width nile green floristry tape. Smooth and polish the taped stem by rubbing with the sides of a pair of scissors. Dust the stem with foliage and vine green. Add a dark patch of lilac-aubergine colouring at the back of the flower where the petals join.

## BUDS

**10** Insert a hooked 18-gauge wire into the base of a long cone of white paste. Neaten the join between the bud and the wire. Divide the surface into three sections using the plain-edge cutting wheel.

**11** Roll out some white paste and cut out six small petals using one of the smaller sage leaf cutters. Soften and vein as for the flower. Attach onto the sides of the bud using fresh egg white. Pinch the tips. Add extra wired petals if desired. Dust as for the flower.

## LEAVES

**12** Florists often use the leaves to create rolled or fan like displays within an arrangement. With this in mind I decided to wire the leaves into fan shapes making them much easier to add to my sugar display.

**13** Roll out some green paste leaving a thick ridge. Cut out a free-hand leaf shape or use a very large rose petal cutter. Insert a moistened 22- or 20-gauge wire into the ridge. Vein using the large nasturtium leaf veiner. Roll or fold the leaf as required. Allow to dry a little before colouring.

**14** Dust in layers with forest, foliage and vine green. Add tinges of lilac to the edges. Spray with edible spray varnish. Allow to dry. These leaves can then be used to fill spaces around the lotus flower spray or taped together to form a complete lily pad shape with a bit of artistic licence thrown in for good measure.

# Hibiscus

*There are many species of hibiscus as well as hybrid forms. Sadly the real flowers only last for one day — at least a sugar version will have a longer lifespan — fingers crossed!!!*

### Materials

*24-, 26- and 33-or 35-gauge white wires*
*White and holly/ivy flowerpaste*
*Plum, fuchsia, daffodil, sunflower, foliage, vine green, forest and aubergine petal dusts*
*Clear alcohol*
*White seed head stamens*
*White and nile green floristry tape*
*Edible spray varnish (Fabilo)*

### Equipment

*Scissors*
*Fine-nose pliers*
*Paintbrush*
*Hibiscus petal and leaf veiners (SKGI)*
*Sharp scalpel*
*Cornflour bag (see page 10)*
*Silk veining tool*
*Rose calyx cutter (OPR11b)*
*Hibiscus leaf veiner (J)*

## PISTIL AND STAMENS

1 Cut five lengths of fine wire – 33-gauge or if you can get hold of some 35 then even better. Bend a tight hook in the end of each wire using fine-nose pliers. Attach a tiny ball of white paste to the end of each hook.

2 Tape the five lengths of wire together using quarter-width white floristry tape curving the tips of each anther back slightly and leaving a little length of each wire exposed. Paint the anthers with a mixture of plum petal dust and clear alcohol.

3 Next, work a piece of white flowerpaste down the length of the wire to approximately the length of the hibiscus petal veiner. Smooth the paste between your palms and curve the whole length slightly. The next step needs to be carried out quickly before the paste starts to dry out – cut lots of short lengths of white

seed-head stamens. Moisten and insert each stamen into the paste just below the curved anthers. The number of stamens varies between varieties. Allow to dry. Dust the length of paste with a mixture of plum and fuchsia petal dusts. Dust the tips of the stamens with a mixture of daffodil and sunflower.

## PETALS

4 Roll out some white flowerpaste, leaving a thick ridge for the wire. Press the flat side of the hibiscus petal veiner against the paste to leave an outline. Cut around the outline with a sharp scalpel or plain-edge cutting wheel. Insert a moistened 26-gauge wire into the ridge. Dust the petal with cornflour and place into the hibiscus petal veiner to texture the petal. You will find that this veiner has a habit of cutting the edges of the petal slightly and that you will need to overlap these cuts and press with your finger to repair them.

**5** Frill the edges of the petal using the silk veining tool. Pinch the petal from the base to the tip and curve slightly to dry. Repeat to make five petals.

**6** Tape the five petals around the base of the pistil using half-width nile green floristry tape. It is best to do this while the petals are still slightly soft so that you can reshape them.

**7** Dust the base of each petal with a mixture of plum and fuchsia.

## CALYX

**8** There are two layers of calyx to this flower. The first layer is cut out from green flowerpaste using a rose calyx cutter. Broaden each sepal using the smooth end of the silk veining tool. Pinch each of the five sepals and thread onto the back of the flower so that each petal has a sepal attached fairly tightly to it. I tend to wire each of the ten outer sepals onto 35- or 33-gauge wire; work a small amount of green flowerpaste onto a wire so that it covers about 2.5 cm (1 in) of the wire. Smooth and flatten the sepal. Pinch and curve into shape with your fingers. Repeat to make ten and tape onto the base of the first calyx. Dust with foliage and vine green.

## BUD

**9** Insert a hooked 24-gauge wire into the base of a cone of holly/ivy coloured flowerpaste. Divide the cone into five sections to represent the inner calyx. Pinch the bud into a sharp point and form a single ridge down the centre of each sepal. Add ten wired sepals as for the calyx on the flower.

## LEAVES

**10** Roll out some green flowerpaste leaving a ridge. Cut out the leaf using the hibiscus leaf veiner. Insert a moistened 26-gauge wire into the ridge. Soften the edges and vein using the leaf veiner. Pinch to accentuate the central vein.

**11** Dust in layers of forest, foliage and vine green. Add tinges of aubergine if desired. Allow to dry and then glaze using spray varnish.

# Gloriosa lily

*This unusual green Gloriosa lily was copied from an Ikebana flower-arranging book that my Japanese friend Fumi gave me. The petals are very much slimmer than the more popular flame red and yellow varieties.*

### STAMENS

**1** Cut six lengths of 33- or 30-gauge white wire. Wrap a small ball of well-kneaded white flowerpaste around a dry wire. Work the paste between your finger and thumb to create the required length – which should be no longer than the length of the petals. The filaments are quite fleshy at the base, tapering into a finer point at the tip. Smooth the filament between your palms and then curve the length. Repeat to make six. Add a small sausage shaped piece of white flowerpaste to represent the anther onto the tip of each filament. Mark a line down the length of each using either a sharp scalpel or plain-edge cutting wheel. Dust the anthers with a mixture sunflower and daffodil. Lightly dust the filaments with a mixture of vine green and edelweiss.

| Materials | Equipment |
|---|---|
| *White, vine green and holly/ivy flowerpaste* | *Sharp scalpel or plain-edge cutting wheel (PME)* |
| *22-, 24-, 26-, 28-, 30- and 33-gauge white wires* | *Lily petal template, see page 142* |
| *Vine green, edelweiss, sunflower, daffodil, foliage,* | *Stargazer B petal veiner (SKGI)* |
| *forest and moss green petal dusts* | *Silk veining tool (HP)* |
| *Nile green floristry tape* | *Plain-edge tweezers* |
| *Edible spray varnish or half glaze* | |

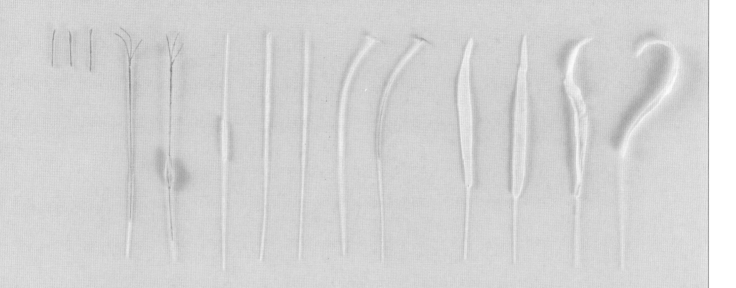

## PISTIL AND OVARY

**2** Twist a length of quarter-width nile green floristry tape back onto itself to create a long strand. Cut three short lengths and tape onto the end of a 30- or 28-gauge white wire using more quarter-width tape. Curl the tips. Add a ball of pale vine green flowerpaste at the base of the pistil, form it into an oval shape and divide into three sections using the scalpel. Pinch a ridge down each section. Dust with moss and vine green. Spray lightly with edible spray varnish. Tape the six stamens around the base of the ovary.

## PETALS

**3** Roll out some pale vine green flowerpaste leaving a fine ridge for the wire. Using the plain-edge cutting wheel or sharp scalpel, cut out the petal freehand or refer to the template on page 142.

**4** Insert a moistened 28-gauge wire into the thick ridge so that the wire is about a third of the way into the petal. Soften the edge and then vein using the Stargazer B petal veiner. Frill the edges of the petal using the silk veining tool – this can be done against your index finger or against a non-stick board.

**5** Pinch the petal from the base to the tip to accentuate a slight central vein and to give the petal its characteristic curve. Pinch the base of the petal with the plain-edge tweezers to leave a narrow, almost triangular, ridge. Re-curl the petal and allow to dry a little before dusting. Repeat to make six petals.

## COLOURING

**6** Dust the petals with a light mixture of daffodil, vine green and edelweiss. Tape the petals around the stamens using half-width tape. Add an extra 22-gauge wire for extra support. Bend the main stem through the petals and straighten up slightly.

## LEAVES

**7** The leaves are generally quite long with a tip that forms into a tendril that the plant uses to cling onto other plants for support. The foliage is not essential – florists will often just use the flowers. The leaves can be made using holly/ivy flowerpaste but they are very fragile. Use 26- or 24-gauge wires depending on the size you are making. I have textured the leaf using several 33-gauge wires pressed together into the surface of the leaf. Dust the leaf in layers with foliage, a touch of forest, moss and vine green. Spray with edible spray varnish.

# Sprays and arrangements

# $\mathcal{F}$lirty floral arrangement

*I have used a collection of some of my favourite flowers and foliage. Flowers are huge flirts and are often hard to resist combining together into colourful arrangements – this is just one of those arrangements!*

### Flowers

*3 white dillenia flowers (see pages 56–9)*
*5 stems of pink dancing ladies ginger (see page 30)*
*1 stem green gloriosa lily (see pages 80–1)*
*5 polyalthia flowers (see page 32)*
*12 dillenia leaves (see page 59)*
*5 rosette succulents (see page 16)*

### Equipment

*20- and 22-gauge wires*
*Nile green floristry tape*
*Florists' staysoft*
*Turquoise glass dish*
*Wire cutters*
*Fine-nose pliers*

## PREPARATION

1 Tape extra 22- or 20-gauge wires onto the flower or leaf stems that require extra support using half-width nile green floristry tape.

2 Take a piece of florists' staysoft and form it into a ball. You might need to put it in a warm place to soften it a little first. Press the staysoft against the glass dish to secure it in place.

## ASSEMBLY

3 Form the focal area of the arrangement with the three dillenia flowers. Use wire cutters to trim each stem if needed and then fine-nose pliers to bend a hook in the end of each flower stem to help support their weight in the staysoft. Add height and width to the arrangement using the five stems of dancing ladies ginger. Curl their stems to create interesting shapes.

4 Next, add the gloriosa lily stem to the left hand side of the arrangement. Add two groups of polyalthia flowers to the lower area of the arrangement to fill in some of space between the dancing ladies and the dillenia flowers.

5 Finally add the dillenia foliage and rosette succulents to hide the visible staysoft and help frame the focal dillenia flowers. It is usually best at this stage to stand back from the arrangement and look at it again as a whole to decide whether the flowers need any adjusting.

*3*

*4*

*5*

# $\mathcal{P}$ink rose and pearls bouquet

*A slight twist on a traditional pink rose-themed bouquet.*

*I have used succulents to create a nice contrast in texture and form.*

*The string of pearls succulents help soften the edges of the design.*

2

3

4

## PREPARATION

**1** Strengthen any flower stems that require extra support or length using half-width floristry tape and 20- or 22-gauge wire depending on the weight of the flower.

## ASSEMBLY

**2** Tape the two stems of akebia onto either side of the full rose using half-width nile green floristry tape, forming 90-degree bends in the wires to form a handle top the bouquet. One stem should form two-thirds the length of the bouquet, with the other shorter one forming the remaining third. Add the half rose and buds to encircle the focal rose.

**3** Use the various sizes of rosette succulents to fill in the gaps around the focal rose and also extend some of the smaller succulents to the edges of the bouquet. You will need to bend the stems with fine-nose pliers as you work and trim away excess wires using wire cutters or large florists' scissors to cut down the bulk of the bouquet handle.

**4** Add the three dissotis flowers spaced evenly around the focal rose. Finally, add trails of string of pearls succulents to soften the edges of the bouquet and create interesting curves into the design. Tape over the handle with full-width nile green floristry tape. Display in the pink glass vase if desired.

| Flowers | Equipment |
|---|---|
| *2 trailing stems of akebia (see pages 26–7)* | *Nile green floristry tape* |
| *1 pink full rose (see pages 40–3)* | *20- and 22-gauge white wires* |
| *1 pink half rose (see pages 40–3)* | *Fine-nose pliers* |
| *3 pink rosebuds (see page xx)* | *Wire cutters or florists' scissors* |
| *9 rosette succulents in assorted sizes (see page 16)* | *Pink glass vase* |
| *3 purple dissotis flowers (see pages 22–3)* | |
| *7 trails of string of pearls succulents (see page 17)* | |

# $\mathcal{G}$olden michelia spray

*This is the spray of flowers from the top tier of the
Flight of fancy wedding cake on pages 130–31.
Displayed in this decorative black vase it forms
an interesting design in its own right.*

2

### Flowers

*3 stems of pink dancing ladies ginger (see page 30)*
*1 michelia flower (see pages 60–2)*
*7 michelia leaves (see page 62)*
*5 stems of string of pearls succulents (see page 17)*
*3 spathoglottis orchids (see pages 52–3)*

### Equipment

*22-gauge wire*
*Nile green floristry tape*
*Fine-nose pliers*
*Florists' scissors or wire cutters*
*Black onion-shaped vase*

3

## PREPARATION

**1** Tape extra 22-gauge wires onto the flower or leaf stems that require extra support using half-width nile green floristry tape.

**2** Tape three stems of dancing ladies around a single michelia flower using half-width nile green tape. Two of the stems should be longer to create the total length of the spray.

**3** Next encircle the michelia flower with its foliage and add trails of string of pearls succulents to follow the line of the dancing ladies. Add an extra twist of 'pearls' to the side of the spray. As you add each piece you will need to bend the wires to almost a 90-degree angle with fine-nose pliers. Trim away any excess wires using large florists' scissors or wire cutters as you assemble the spray.

**4** Finally add the three spathoglottis orchids to the edges of the spray. Neaten the handle of the spray, taping over with full-width nile green tape. Insert the handle of the spray into the black vase to finish the display.

# Orchid trail bouquet

*This style of bouquet is great fun to construct. The silver and paper-covered wires help to create a strong trailing structure.*

2

## PREPARATION

**1** Strengthen the lotus leaves and orchid stems by taping them onto 22-gauge wires with half-width nile green floristry tape.

## ASSEMBLY

**2** Tape the lotus leaves around the large cymbidium orchid with half-width tape. Add two lengths of silver wire to create the main structure of the bouquet. Curl and curve the wire to create an interesting shape. Trim the wires with wire cutters.

**3** Tape together the small cymbidium orchid and a lotus leaf using half-width tape. Add a milkweed flower using fine-nose pliers to bend the stem at a 90-degree angle and then tape onto the end of the silver wire.

**4** Add the milkweed flowers evenly spaced around the larger cymbidium, taping them in tightly. Next, add the spathoglottis orchids and their buds to the edges of the bouquet.

**5** Finally, add lengths of green- and pink-paper covered wire tangled together to snake through the bouquet and around the main silver wire frame. Display the bouquet in an egg-shaped vase. Reshape the wires accordingly.

4

| Equipment | Flowers |
|---|---|
| *22-gauge wires* | *6 lotus leaves (see page 77)* |
| *Nile green floristry tape* | *2 cymbidium orchids (see pages 72–3)* |
| *Silver wire* | *3 spathoglottis orchids, plus buds (see pages 52–3)* |
| *Wire cutters* | *7 milkweed flowers (see pages 70–1)* |
| *Fine-nose pliers* | |
| *Pink- and green-paper covered wire* | |
| *Egg-shaped vase* | |

# Rose and coffee spray

*This colourful straight spray of flowers from the Coffee aroma cake would also make a pretty keepsake displayed as it is here, in a brightly coloured glass vase.*

### Flowers

*1 full rose (see pages 40–3)*
*8 polyalthia flowers (see page 32)*
*9 polyalthia buds (see page 32)*
*1 twig of coffee cherries (see pages 36–7)*
*9 coffee leaves (see page 37)*
*2 small groups of coffee cherries (see page 37)*
*4 rose buds (see page 40, Step 1)*
*3 coffee flowers (see pages 36–7)*
*3 croton leaves (see page 45)*
*2 stems of red Hawaiian swinging pea (see pages 34–5)*

### Equipment

*Nile green floristry tape*
*Tape shredder*
*22-gauge white wires*
*Fine pliers or strong scissors*
*Wire cutters*

## PREPARATION

**1** Shred some nile green floristry tape into half width using a tape shredder. Strengthen any of the flowers and foliage if required by taping extra 22-gauge wires alongside their main stems.

## ASSEMBLY

**2** Use the full rose as the focal point of the spray, encircling it with the polyalthia flowers and buds – use fine pliers to bend the stems as you add them to help them fit neatly around the rose. Tape together using half-width floristry tape. Add an extended length of polyalthia flowers and buds to form the straight-line structure of the spray.

**3** Next add the twig of coffee cherries and leaves alongside the line of polyalthia. Trim off excess wire stems using wire cutters or large, strong scissors as you work. Add the two small groups of coffee cherries around the top edge of the spray and pull in the four rose buds around the main focal rose.

**4** Add the coffee flowers and fill in the outer edge of the spray with the croton leaves and remaining coffee leaves. Finally add the two stems of red swinging pea flowers opposite each other on either side of the focal rose. Neaten the handle of the spray by taping over with full-width floristry tape. Display in a colourful glass vase.

2

3

4

# Oncoba arrangement

*I have combined a mixture of flowers and fruit to create this unusual arrangement of flowers. The African oncoba flower forms the focal point of the display with its oddly shaped fruit, with the sharp orange coloured kumquats and coffee fruit adding extra interest to the design.*

### Flowers

*1 stem of coffee flowers and foliage (see pages 36–7)*
*1 stem of coffee cherries and foliage (see pages 36–7)*
*1 oncoba flower (see pages 67–9)*
*7 oncoba leaves (see page 69)*
*1 oncoba fruit (see page 69)*
*3 rothmania flowers and 2 buds (see pages 24–5)*
*5 kumquat fruit, plus foliage (see page 31)*

### Equipment

*22- and 26-gauge green or white wires*
*Nile green floristry tape*
*Wire cutters*
*Broad green organza ribbon*
*Green florists' staysoft*
*Green glass tea-light holder*
*Green beaded wire*
*Fine-nose pliers*

## PREPARATION

**1** Start by adding extra 22-gauge wire with half-width nile green floristry tape to any of the stems that require extra length or support. Form a loop of broad green organza ribbon and secure using a 26-gauge wire and floristry tape.

**2** Firmly press a ball of florists' staysoft into the tea-light holder to secure it in place. Create a 'necklace' of the green beaded wire and position it around the top edge of the container.

## ASSEMBLY

**3** Using fine-nose pliers bend a hook in the ends of both coffee flower and fruit stems to help support their weight in the arrangement. Insert them into the staysoft and curve to form an 'S' shape.

**4** Add the oncoba flower to create the focal point of the arrangement. Encircle the flower with its own foliage and add the fruit to hang towards the base of the arrangement.

**5** Next, add a line to the left-hand side of the arrangement using the Rothmania flowers and buds. Add the kumquats grouped opposite each other in the arrangement on either side of the oncoba flower.

**6** Finally add the organza ribbon loop at the back of the arrangement.

# Trail blazer bouquet

*A plaited extended trail of paper-covered wire forms an interesting framework for this unusual bouquet of succulents, auricula and fiddle-head ferns.*

## PREPARATION

**1** Tape 24- or 22-gauge wire onto any of the flower and foliage stems that require extra support or length.

## ASSEMBLY

**2** Cut three lengths of aubergine and two lengths of green paper-covered wire. Loosely plait the wire together to form one very long or two shorter plaits. Bend the wire to create a long trail and complete with a loop to form the outline of the bouquet.

**3** Place the large aubergine coloured succulent at the centre of the bouquet to create the focal point. Complete a line of these succulents by adding the other two smaller ones on either side. Next, fill in around this area with the green rosettes. Trim off excess wires with wire cutters as you work to cut down on some of the bulk of the handle. Two of the smaller green rosettes have been taped onto longer wires to enable them to be threaded into the long plaited trail – you will need to use fine-nose pliers to help you thread and pull these into the bouquet.

**4** Next, fill the gaps using the auricula flowers and leaves – try to keep these slightly recessed in the bouquet. Add the curls of fiddle-head fern to the edges of the bouquet and finally wrap and trail the strings of pearls around the plaited framework to soften the edges. Neaten the handle with full-width nile green floristry tape.

|  |  |  |
|---|---|---|
| **Flowers** | **Equipment** | *2* |
| *1 large and 2 smaller dark aubergine rosette succulents (see page 16)* | *22- and 24-gauge wires* | |
| *7 green rosette succulents in assorted sizes (see page 16)* | *Aubergine and green paper-covered wire* | |
| *7 auricula flowers (see pages 38–9)* | *Wire cutters* | |
| *9 auricula leaves in assorted sizes (see page 39)* | *Fine-nose pliers* | |
| *7 fiddle-head ferns (see page 44)* | *Nile green floristry tape* | |
| *5 trails of string of pearls succulent (see page 17)* | | |

3

4

# $\mathcal{S}$ingapore sling floral spray

*These pretty orchids are very simple to arrange into*

*this delicate spray. Dried dyed natural leaves and*

*beaded wire help to soften the edges of the spray.*

3

## PREPARATION

**1** Wire the dried aqua leaves onto 28-gauge wire using half-width nile green floristry tape. Cut lengths of beaded wire with wire cutters or sharp scissors. Bend over the ends of each wire using fine-nose pliers to prevent the beads escaping. Add 24-gauge wire onto any of the flower, bud or leaf stems that might require extra length or support.

## ASSEMBLY

**2** Form the basic outline of the spray using the pumpkin seed succulents – bend each stem to a 90-degree angle and tape together to form a handle to the spray. The spray needs to be measured in thirds so one stem should be two-thirds the length required for the spray and the other stem forming the remaining third.

**3** Add the three sets of orchid buds and two orchids to fill in more of the outline.

**4** Fill in the remaining gaps with more orchids – adding one at the centre as the focal flower.

**5** Add curls of aqua beaded wire, taping each length in turn into the spray with half-width nile green floristry tape. Add a long trail to use as the extension for the smaller spray of flowers.

**6** Add the dried aqua leaves to both fill in and soften the edges of the spray. Tape together two orchids with a few buds plus some succulents to form a smaller spray. Tape onto the end of the beaded wire.

4

| **Flowers** | **Equipment** |
|---|---|
| *8 stems of pumpkin seed succulents (see page 17)* | *Aqua coloured dried leaves* |
| *3 sets of spathoglottis buds (see page 53)* | *24- and 28-gauge white wires* |
| *7 spathoglottis orchids (see pages 52–3)* | *Nile green floristry tape* |
| | *Wire cutters or sharp scissors* |
| | *Fine-nose pliers* |
| | *Aqua beaded wire* |

# $\mathcal{E}$xotic white wedding bouquet

*The arched fragile stems of the Brassia orchids and the gold swirls of paper-covered wire help soften the edges of the bold Dillenia flowers and foliage. This type of bouquet is fairly simple to construct.*

*3*

*4*

### PREPARATION

**1** Strengthen any flower stems or foliage that might need it by taping 22-, 20- or 18-gauge wire onto their main stems – the gauge will depend on the weight of the item. I tend to use either half- or full-width floristry tape when wiring together larger bouquets.

### ASSEMBLY

**2** Bend the two long brassia orchids bud stems to a 90 degree angle using fine-nose pliers and tape them together using full-width nile green floristry tape. Curve the stems to create a large crescent shape. Next, add the dillenia flower to create the focal point of the bouquet. Add two of the brassia orchids onto either side of the dillenia at the base of the orchid buds. Add the remaining brassia orchid to help balance the display.

**3** Next, add the Dillenia buds in two groups opposite each other in the bouquet. Cut off excess stem as you work using wire cutters or strong scissors; this cuts down on some of the bulk around the handle of the bouquet making it easier to insert into a posy pick.

**4** Use the Dillenia leaves and glossy green berries to fill in the large gaps of the bouquet. Add extended lengths of gold paper-covered wire to complete the display. Curl the wires as you add them to create a pleasing free flowing shape.

### FOR THE GLOSSY BERRIES

These are not based on any one particular species – they are just great space fillers that are quick and easy to make. Bend a hook in the end of a beige wire, roll a ball of pale green flowerpaste. Moisten the wire and pull it through the berry, leaving part of the hook showing. Smooth the berry onto the wire to form a more pleasing oval shape. Dust brightly with vine and foliage green. Spray heavily with edible spray varnish to give a good gloss.

| Flowers | Equipment |
|---|---|
| *2 brassia orchid bud stems (see page 55)* | *18-, 20- and 22-gauge wire* |
| *1 white dillenia flower (see pages 56–9)* | *Nile green floristry tape* |
| *3 single brassia orchids (see pages 54–5)* | *Wire cutters or strong scissors* |
| *5 dillenia buds (see page 59)* | *Fine-nose pliers* |
| *9 dillenia leaves (see page 59)* | *Gold paper-covered wire* |
| *2 groups of glossy green berries* | |

# Moroccan dream

*A very novel creation of gloriosa, kumquats and succulents arranged in an upturned tagine lid! This is one of my favourite arrangements in this book. It can be fun trying to find unusual containers for sugar flowers – this arrangement has a sort of windswept quality to it. In fact some heavy-duty Blu Tack might be needed to stop this oddity flying away.*

*1*

**1** Fill the tagine lid with florists' staysoft. Trim the gloriosa lily stem with wire cutters and bend a large open hook in the end using fine-nose pliers. Insert the stem into the staysoft to form the focal feature of the arrangement.

**2** Next add the succulents to cover the base of the arrangement and the staysoft.

**3** Finally add the two stems of kumquat.

*3*

| **Flowers** | **Equipment** |
| --- | --- |
| *1 green gloriosa lily, plus foliage (see pages 80–1)* | *Blue tagine lid* |
| *5 rosette succulents (see page 16)* | *Florists' staysoft* |
| *2 stems of kumquat (see page 31)* | *Wire cutters* |
| | *Fine-nose pliers* |

# $\mathscr{G}$olden days

*Climbing stems of golden snake vine flowers and foliage have been arranged into an unusual oak burr container combined with plaited lengths of gold, brown and beige paper-covered wire to form a stylish upright arrangement. Florists' staysoft has been used inside the container to hold the flowers firmly in place. The container was then filled with dried mung beans to form a decorative cover over the mechanics of the arrangement – other dried food ingredients work well too – coffee, lentils, peas, etc.*

1 Strengthen the trailing stems if necessary, taping extra 18-gauge wire onto the existing stems using half-width nile green floristry tape. Plait together a few lengths of brown, gold and beige paper covered wire. Curl and curve the lengths to create interesting shapes.

2 Press a lump of kneaded florists' staysoft into the base of the oak burr container.

3 Trim the stems if required using wire cutters. Bend a hook in the end of each stem just before you press the stem into the staysoft – the hooks will help to give the stems a little more support.

4 Gradually add the lengths of plaited paper-covered wire to snake its way through the arrangement. Curve the stems of snake vine to form an attractive shape.

*4*

---

**Flowers**

*3 stems of snake vine flowers, buds and foliage*
*(see pages 64–6)*

**Equipment**

*18-gauge white wires*
*Nile green floristry tape*
*Brown, gold and beige paper-covered wire*
*Florists' staysoft*
*Oak burr container (or similar)*
*Wire cutters*
*Fine-nose pliers*
*Dried mung beans*

# $\mathcal{L}$otus arrangement

*I am always on the lookout for containers, vases and candleholders to help display my flowers. This container lives in Sue Atkinson's (the photographer) props cupboard! Its lush green colour works really well as a base for the brightly coloured lotus, paphia and trailing pea flowers.*

1 Add extra 18-gauge wire to the lotus stems if they need extra support, using half-width nile green floristry tape. Fill the container with green florists' staysoft.

2 Trim the ends of the lotus stems using wire cutters. Bend a hook in the end of each stem just before you embed it into the staysoft – this will give extra support to the heavier flowers. Create a line of colour using the open lotus flower and the two buds. Add the group of five paphia flowers to the right-hand edge of the container so that they hang their heads over the edge.

3 Next add the two stems of trailing peas so that they, too, hang gracefully at the right-hand side of the arrangement.

4 Finally add the folded lotus leaves to fill in gaps behind the lotus flowers. Stand back from the arrangement to take an overview of it and then carefully curve and bend any flower stems that might require it to create a more pleasing overall finish.

| Flowers | Equipment |
|---|---|
| *1 open lotus flower, 1 half open bud and 1 tight bud (see pages 75–7)* | *18-gauge white wire* |
| *5 paphia flowers, plus foliage (see page 33)* | *Nile green floristry tape* |
| *2 stems of Hawaiian swinging pea (see pages 34–5)* | *Green container* |
| *7 folded lotus leaves (see page 77)* | *Green florists' staysoft* |
| | *Wire cutters* |
| | *Pliers* |

# Gone to seed

*This is a small arrangement of swinging Hawaiian pea pods and cream milkweed flowers that could be used on top of a cake if desired or as a fun table decoration. Sometimes simple combinations of flowers work best.*

**1** Using the wire cutters, trim the stems of the milkweed and the pods if required to shorten the stems suitably to fit into the vase.

**2** Using fine-nose pliers bend the stems of the swinging pea pods to hook onto the side of the vase.

**3** Next, group together the milkweed flowers and buds to form a cluster. Tape them together with half-width nile green floristry tape. Insert the stem into the top of the vase, and then carefully re-arrange the flowers to 'relax' them into place

---

**Flowers**

*5 milkweed flowers, plus buds (see pages 70–1)*

*3 Hawaiian swinging pea pods (see pages 34–5)*

**Equipment**

*Wire cutters*

*Fine-nose pliers*

*Nile green floristry tape.*

*Small apple shaped vase*

Cakes

# Siamese cat

*This wonderful Siamese cat design was taken from a greetings card. The original watercolour is by artist Kay Stoddard who I managed to contact via the card company The Medici Society to ask her permission to use the design in this book – she very kindly agreed.*

## Materials

*23-cm (9-in) round rich fruitcake*
*Apricot glaze*
*1 kg (2 lb 3 oz) white almond paste*
*1.5 kg (3 lb 5 oz) white sugarpaste*
*Icing sugar*
*Clear alcohol (Cointreau or kirsch)*
*Fine soft lavender blue ribbon, to trim the cake*
*Broad soft lavender blue ribbon, to trim the board*
*Non-toxic glue stick (Pritt)*
*Small amount of cocoa butter (SK)*
*Lavender, bluebell, edelweiss, nutkin brown, black, sunflower, African violet, plum and deep purple petal dusts*
*Nile green floristry tape*

## Equipment

*Pastry brush*
*Sugarpaste smoothers*
*33-cm (13-in) round cake board*
*Curved rose embosser (Fmm)*
*Cat design, see template on page 112*
*Greaseproof paper or tracing paper*
*Sharp pencil*
*Cake scriber or biro that has run dry*
*Mug and saucer*
*Selection of paintbrushes*
*Sharp scalpel*

## Flowers

*2 trailing stems of tweedia, plus a few extra flowers and leaves (see pages 28–9)*
*3 dissotis flowers, plus foliage (see pages 22–3)*
*3 sprigs of akebia flowers, plus foliage (see pages 26–7)*

## PREPARATION

**1** Brush the cake with warmed apricot glaze and cover with almond paste. Leave to dry at least overnight. Roll out the sugarpaste on a fine dusting of icing sugar. Moisten the surface of the almond paste with clear alcohol and cover with sugarpaste using sugarpaste smoothers to create a good finish.

**2** Cover the cake board with white sugarpaste and position the cake centrally on top. Add a decorative border around the edge of the board using the curved heart embosser. Allow to dry overnight.

**3** Attach a band of fine lavender blue ribbon around the base of the cake using a small amount of royal icing or sugarpaste softened with clear alcohol. Tie a small bow of ribbon and position at the base. Use a non-toxic glue stick to attach the broader ribbon to the edge of the cake board.

## COCOA PAINTED DESIGN

**4** Trace the cat design on page 112 onto tracing or greaseproof paper using a sharp pencil. Place the tracing on top of the cake and scribe the design carefully onto the surface of the cake – using a cake scriber or better still a biro pen that has run out of ink.

**5** Place a small amount of grated/shaved cocoa butter onto a saucer and place over a mug of just boiled water to melt it. Add small amounts of petal dust to the melted cocoa butter to make a paint. Carefully paint in the design of the cat and bubbles. Start by painting in the design with very pale colours gradually building up and adding extra detail in layers. You might find that you will have to allow a short length of time between layers to allow the cocoa butter to set. Use a sharp scalpel to etch away fine detail lines for the whiskers and highlight in the eyes, etc.

**6** Using nile green floristry tape, tape together the flowers and foliage to create a crescent shape spray. Use the two longer tweedia stems as the main structure frame for the spray. Fill in the focal area using the dissotis flowers surrounded by the

# ⊤rail blazer

*Auriculas with their wonderful, subtle colours help to soften the almost architectural form of the fleshy rosette succulents. The extended trail of plaited paper-covered wire and curls of fern help to create a very unusual wedding cake design.*

## PREPARATION

**1** Mix together equal amounts of champagne and white sugarpaste to produce an off-white paste. Leave to rest.

**2** Place the small cake onto a thin cake board of the same size. Brush both cakes with warmed apricot glaze and cover each with almond paste. Leave to dry overnight.

**3** Roll out the sugarpaste on a fine dusting of icing sugar. Moisten the surface of the almond paste with clear alcohol and cover both cakes separately with the sugarpaste, using sugarpaste smoothers to create a good finish. Cover the cake board with paste and transfer the large cake to sit centrally on top. Place the smaller cake on top of the base tier.

## RIBBON

**4** To match the colour of the flowers I used a mixture of plum and aubergine to dust the cream sections of the green and cream braid I had bought. Attach to the base of both cakes using a small amount of royal icing or sugarpaste softened with clear alcohol.

**5** Use the broad velvet ribbon to trim the large board using the non-toxic glue stick to hold it securely.

**6** Tape together the bouquet as described on pages 96–7, plus a smaller corsage to sit at the side of the baseboard. Insert the posy pick into the top tier and position the handle of the spray into it. Adjust the flowers and foliage if necessary to complete the design.

### Materials

*750 g (1 lb 10 oz) champagne sugarpaste*
*750 g (1 lb 10 oz) white sugarpaste*
*13-cm (5-in) and 20-cm (8-in) round rich fruitcakes*
*Apricot glaze*
*1 kg (2 lb 3 oz) almond paste*
*Clear alcohol (Cointreau or kirsch)*
*Icing sugar*
*Cream/green ribbon braid, to trim the cakes*
*Plum and aubergine petal dusts*
*Broad green velvet ribbon, to trim the cakeboard*

### Equipment

*13-cm (5-in) round thin cake board*
*13-cm (5-in) round thin cake board*
*30-cm (12-in) round cake board*
*Sugarpaste smoothers*
*Dusting brush*
*Non-toxic glue stick (Pritt)*
*Posy pick (W)*
*Nile green floristry tape*

### Flowers

*1 trail blazer bouquet (see pages 96–7)*
*2 rosette succulents (see page 16)*
*2 short stems of string of pearls (see page 17)*

# Coffee cake

### Materials

*20-cm (8-in) teardrop-shaped rich fruitcake*
*Apricot glaze*
*750 g (1 lb 10 oz) white almond paste*
*Icing sugar*
*Clear alcohol (Cointreau or kirsch)*
*1 kg (2 lb 3 oz) white sugarpaste*
*Fine 'nude' ribbon, to trim the cake*
*Broad 'nude' ribbon, to trim the board*
*Non-toxic glue stick (Pritt)*
*Peach, ivory and white rice/wafer paper*
*Piping gel*
*28-gauge white wire*
*Nile green floristry tape*

### Equipment

*Pastry brush*
*Large non-stick rolling pin*
*Sugarpaste smoothers*
*30-cm (12-in) teardrop shaped cake board*
*Sharp fine scissors*
*Food grade plastic posy pick*

### Flowers

*1 rose and coffee spray (see pages 92–3)*

*Although I have used roses as the focal flowers on this cake it was actually the coffee flowers and fruit that were the initial inspiration. The simple but effective abstract rose design around the base of the cake has been created using strips of curled rice paper. I love decorating fruitcakes — they are firmer to decorate than sponge cakes — but perhaps here a coffee flavoured cake would be a good choice?*

## PREPARATION

1 Brush the cake with warmed apricot glaze. Roll out the almond paste using a large non-stick rolling pin on a fine dusting of icing sugar. Cover the cake, trim away the excess and smooth over the surface using sugarpaste smoothers. Allow to dry overnight at least.

2 Moisten the surface of the almond paste with clear alcohol and cover with the sugarpaste. Sugarpaste smoothers are essential to create a good covering, however, the tight curl of the teardrop shaped cake can be problematic – this is where I favour smoothing the edges and surface of the cake with a pad of well-kneaded sugarpaste pressed firmly into the palm to polish the surface. Cover the cake board with sugarpaste and transfer the cake on top. Use smoothers again to blend the join between the cake and the board. Allow to dry.

3 Attach a band of fine ribbon around the base of the cake using a small dot of softened sugarpaste to hold it in place. Attach the broader ribbon to the board edge using the non-toxic glue stick.

## RICE PAPER CURLS

4 Cut thin strips of peach, ivory and white rice/wafer paper using a sharp pair of scissors – vary the width and length of the strips. Carefully roll and curl each strip of rice paper back onto itself to create a mixture of tight and loosely curled rose-like formations. Cut several small freehand rose leaves from the ivory rice paper to soften the edges of the design. Attach to the base of the cake and board using tiny amounts of piping gel or simply scatter the curls around the cake board just before the cake goes on display.

5 Wire the spray of flowers with white wire, then add trails of fine ribbon to the spray. Tape over and add to the spray using half-width nile green floristry tape.

6 Insert the posy pick into the cake and position the handle of the spray into it. Carefully re-arrange the flowers if necessary to enhance and relax the overall effect.

# Bucks fizz

*I love using bright colours together – here I have used bright kumquat oranges, pink pavonia and mock orange flowers to create this very vibrant cocktail party of a birthday cake!*

## PREPARATION

**1** Brush the cake with warmed apricot glaze and cover with white almond paste. Leave to dry overnight. Brush the surface with clear alcohol and cover with pale pink sugarpaste. Smooth the surface with sugarpaste smoothers. Cover the cake board with pink sugarpaste and transfer the cake on top. Use the smoothers to help blend the join between the cake and the board.

**2** Quickly press the dragéées in the sugarpaste, coating at intervals around the cake – you might prefer to use a tiny amount of royal icing to help hold them in place. Attach a band of silver ribbon around the base of the board, securing it either with a small amount of royal icing or sugarpaste softened with clear alcohol. Glue a band of soft lime ribbon to the edge of the board using the non-toxic glue stick.

## SIDE DESIGN

**3** Add painted details around the embedded dragéées using a mixture of Cointreau and petal dusts. I have used plum and tangerine to add spots and petals around each of the dragéées and a mixture of vine green and foliage to add a few tiny leaves to the design.

## SPRAYS

**4** Tape together two sprays of flowers using half-width nile green floristry tape – one spray needs to be much smaller than the other. Use the mock orange flowers grouped together to create the focal point of the sprays and add the other flowers and foliage around them to create a curved shape. Add curls of silver paper-covered wire and aqua beaded wire to extended the length and shape.

**5** Insert the posy pick into the cake and then position the spray into it. Curl the wires around the cake to create a pleasing effect. Tape together a small spray of flowers, adding a butterfly to complete it. Position the butterfly at the base of the cake, either resting against the cake or push a fine posy pick into the base of the cake to hold the handle of the spray.

## BUTTERFLY

**6** To make the basic shape of the butterfly follow the instructions on page 140. I have dusted this butterfly with bluegrass and vine green mixed together followed by a mixture of plum and white petal dusts. The body, antennae and detail on the wings have been painted using a mixture of black petal dust and alcohol. Allow the black to dry and then highlight with bridal satin spots and flecks.

## Materials

*20-cm (8-in) teardrop shaped fruitcake*
*Apricot glaze*
*750 g (1 lb 10 oz) white almond paste*
*Clear alcohol (Cointreau or kirsch)*
*1 kg (2 lb 3 oz) pale pink sugarpaste*
*Edible metallic-effect dragéées*
*Royal icing (optional)*
*Fine silver ribbon, to trim the cake*
*Broad soft lime ribbon, to trim the cake*
*Non-toxic craft glue stick (Pritt)*
*Plum, tangerine, vine green, foliage, bluegrass, white, black and bridal satin petal dusts*
*Nile green floristry tape*
*Silver paper-covered wire*
*Aqua coloured beaded wire*

## Equipment

*Pastry brush*
*Sugarpaste smoother*
*30-cm (12-in) teardrop shaped cake board*
*Assorted fine paintbrushes*
*Posy pick*
*Fine posy pick (Cc)*
*Butterfly cutters (Jem), or see template on page 143*
*Sharp scalpel*
*Isopropyl alcohol*

## Flowers

*4 mock orange flowers, plus foliage and buds (see pages 20–1)*
*4 kumquats, plus foliage (see page 31)*
*5 paphia flowers (see page 33)*
*3 pavonia flowers in varying sizes (see pages 50–1)*
*1 exotic fantasy butterfly (see page 140)*

# Singapore sling

## Materials

*12.5 cm (5 in) round rich fruitcake*
*Apricot glaze*
*450 g (1 lb) white almond paste*
*Icing sugar*
*450 g (1 lb) white sugarpaste*
*Clear alcohol (Cointreau or kirsch)*
*Small amount of cocoa butter*
*White, plum, African violet and bluegrass petal dusts*
*Fine lavender coloured ribbon*
*Broad pink organza ribbon*
*Posy pick*

## Equipment

*12.5 cm (5 in) thin cake board*
*Pastry brush*
*Rolling pin*
*Straight-edge sugarpaste smoother*
*Rounded sugarpaste smoother*
*18 cm (7 in) round white metal base*
*Heart template, see page 142*
*Saucer and mug*
*Fine paintbrushes*

## Flowers

*1 Singapore sling spray (see pages 120–21)*

*Several years ago I visited the botanical gardens in Singapore. When no one was looking I picked a few of these pretty little spathoglottis orchids as samples to work from only to find that outside the garden gates the exact same orchids were growing like weeds!*

### PREPARATION

**1** Place the cake onto a thin cake board the same size. Brush with warmed apricot glaze. Roll out the almond paste onto a light dusting of icing sugar and cover the cake and the depth of the board too. Remove the excess paste using a cutting/scraping action with the side of a straight-edge sugarpaste smoother. Allow to dry overnight.

**2** Roll out some white sugarpaste on a dusting of icing sugar. Quickly moisten the surface of the almond paste with clear alcohol and cover with the sugarpaste. Use the rounded smoother on the top of the cake and then the straight-edge smoother on the sides. Polish the whole cake with a pad of sugarpaste pressed into your palm. Attach the cake to the larger round white metal base using a small amount of sugarpaste softened with clear alcohol. Allow to dry overnight.

### SIDE DESIGN

**3** I have painted the heart design onto the side of the cake using a freehand technique. However, I have included a template on page 143 if you would prefer to

scribe the design into the surface first. Melt a small amount of cocoa butter onto a saucer held over a mug of just boiled water. Add white and plum petal dusts to a small amount of the melted cocoa butter to form a paint. Using a fine paintbrush paint the heart design at intervals around the sides of the cake. Allow the paint to set slightly before increasing the amount of plum petal dust and adding a tiny amount of African violet too. Darken one half of each heart using this mixture. Using a clean, fine brush add spots of bluegrass mixed with white petal dusts and cocoa butter to soften the edges of the heart design.

**4** Attach a band of fine lavender ribbon around the base of the cake using a small amount of sugarpaste softened with clear alcohol. Attach a broader band of pink organza ribbon over the top.

**5** Construct the spray following the instructions on pages 120–21 for the Singapore sling spray. Insert the handle of the spray into the posy pick and then into the cake. Trail and rest the smaller section of the spray against the base board.

*1*

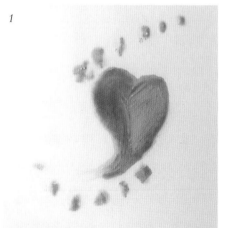

# *E*xotic white wedding cake

*White and green flowers always give an instantly fresh bridal feel to a cake. Exotic white Dillenia and green Brassia orchids combine with gold hearts and swirls to create a very modern design.*

## PREPARATION

**1** Place the small cake onto the oval cake board of the same size. Brush both cakes with warmed apricot glaze and then cover with white almond paste. Leave to dry overnight. Roll out the sugarpaste on a fine dusting of icing sugar. Moisten the surface with clear alcohol and cover with the sugarpaste. Use sugarpaste smoothers to achieve a good finish. Moisten the surface of the larger oval cake board and cover with the sugarpaste. Transfer the large cake on top of the coated board.

**2** Place the small cake off set on top of the base tier. Use a sugarpaste smoother to apply pressure to form a neat bond between the two cakes. Allow the cakes to dry overnight if time allows.

**3** Attach a thin band of pale lemon ribbon around the base of each cake, securing it in place with a small amount of royal icing or sugarpaste softened with clear alcohol. Glue a band of green velvet ribbon to the board edge using the non-toxic glue stick.

## SIDE DESIGN

**4** Thinly roll out some flowerpaste onto a non-stick board. Turn the paste over to reveal a 'sticky' side and then quickly place a fine sheet of edible gold leaf on top of the paste. Use a clean, dry flat dusting brush to bond the two mediums together; this is not an easy process – gold leaf has a life of its own! Use the plain-edge cutting wheel to create a crosshatch design into the gold leaf paste. While the paste is still soft, cut out some gold hearts using a couple of sizes of curved heart cutters. Attach in pairs around the sides of the cake using a little clear alcohol as glue to hold them in place.

## FLOWERS

**5** Wire up the two flower sprays following the instructions on page 100. Insert two posy picks directly into the wedding cake. Position the handles of each spray into the picks.

### Materials

*15-cm (6-in) and 25-cm (10-in) oval fruitcakes*
*Apricot glaze*
*2.25 kg (5 lb) white almond paste*
*Clear alcohol (Cointreau or kirsch)*
*3 kg (6 lb 10 oz) white sugarpaste*
*Icing sugar*
*Pale lemon ribbon, to trim the cakes*
*Royal icing (optional)*
*Broad green velvet ribbon, to trim the baseboard*
*Small amount of white flowerpaste*
*Edible gold leaf (SK)*

### Equipment

*15-cm (6-in) thin oval cake board*
*25-cm (10-in) oval cake board*
*Pastry brush*
*Sugarpaste smoothers*
*Non-toxic glue stick (Pritt)*
*Flat dusting brush*
*Plain-edge cutting wheel*
*Curved heart cutters (LS)*
*2 posy picks (Wilton)*

### Flowers

*2 exotic white wedding bouquets (see pages 100–01)*

# Orchid trail wedding cake

*I adore orchids. They are unusual, eye-catching and not too difficult to make. This cake design shows trails of wire to connect only two very bold cymbidium orchids together on this dramatic two-tiered wedding cake.*

## PREPARATION

**1** Mix together champagne sugarpaste with some pink paste food colour to achieve an oyster colour – the proportions will depend upon your own taste – I just keep adding small amounts of pink to the champagne until I am happy with the colour. Brush the cakes with warmed apricot glaze. Roll out the almond paste on a fine dusting of icing sugar and cover both cakes. Allow to dry overnight.

**2** Moisten the surface of the cakes with clear alcohol and cover with the oyster coloured sugarpaste. Trim away the excess sugarpaste and smooth the top of the cakes with the curved-edge sugarpaste smoother. Work on the sides with the straight-edge smoother.

**3** Cover both cake boards with oyster sugarpaste and transfer the cakes on top. Blend the join between the cake and the board using the straight-edge smoother. Allow to dry.

**4** Attach a band of fine pink ribbon around the base of both cakes attaching it with a tiny amount of sugarpaste softened with clear alcohol. Glue a band of oyster coloured ribbon around the edge of both boards using the non-toxic craft glue stick.

## SIDE DESIGN

**5** I freehand painted the design onto the cakes – however, you can refer to the template on page 143 if you prefer to scribe it onto the cake first. Melt a small amount of cocoa butter on a saucer above a mug of just boiled water. Mix in some vine green and white petal dusts to form a paint. Using a fine paintbrush, start to form a five-petal blossom onto the surface of the cake. Repeat the blossoms dotted around both cakes. Next add longer oval-shaped pink petals in between the green petals using plum and white petal dusts mixed together with a little more cocoa butter. Darken the mixture with a touch of aubergine and add darker lines to the outer petals and dots for stamens at the heart of the green blossom.

**6** Place the Perspex separator nest onto the large cake and carefully place the small cake on top. Wire up the bouquet on page 90 and insert a posy pick into the top tier to hold the bouquet. Bend and curve the connecting wires to form an attractive trail from the top to the bottom tier.

---

| Materials | Equipment |
|---|---|
| 1.8 kg (4 lb) champagne sugarpaste | Pastry brush |
| Pink paste food colour | Rolling pin |
| 15 cm (6 in) and 25.5 cm (10 in) round rich | Curved-edge sugarpaste smoother |
| fruitcakes | Straight-edge sugarpaste smoother |
| Apricot glaze | 18 cm (7 in) and 35.5 cm (14 in) round cake boards |
| 1.4 kg (3 lb) white almond paste | Flower template, see page 143 |
| Icing sugar | Mug and saucer |
| Clear alcohol (Cointreau or kirsch) | Fine paintbrushes |
| Fine pink ribbon, to trim the cakes | Perspex separator nest (Cc) |
| Broad oyster coloured ribbon | 1 posy pick |
| Non-toxic craft glue stick | |
| Small amount of cocoa butter | **Flowers** |
| Vine green, white, plum and aubergine petal dusts | 1 orchid trail bouquet (see page 90–1) |

# Everlasting love

*The flowers on this cake were originally made for my parents' fortieth wedding anniversary. I have tried to recreate the original cake, which had a delicate piped royal iced embroidery design on the sides and tops of each cake. The template is on page 143 if you wish to use it – I've used part of the design here. This design would also make a wonderful wedding cake.*

## PREPARATION

**1** Colour the sugarpaste using the bluegrass food colour to create a soft aqua colour. I love tilting cakes – however, at the back of my mind I am always worried about the cake falling off the stand! I have used a polystyrene dummy cake as the top tier for this design as it is only decorative. Roll out the sugarpaste on a fine dusting of icing sugar. Moisten the surface of the dummy cake evenly with clear alcohol – dry areas will encourage air bubbles underneath the sugarpaste. Place onto a sheet of greaseproof paper and cover with about one third of the sugarpaste. Use sugarpaste smoothers and then a pad of sugarpaste pressed into your palm to polish the surface of the cake. Trim away excess paste to neaten the base of the cake and leave to dry for a few days.

**2** Brush the large fruitcake with warmed apricot glaze and cover with the white almond paste. Allow to dry. Moisten the surface with clear alcohol and cover with aqua coloured sugarpaste, leaving a little aside to cover the cake board. Cover the cake board with the remaining sugarpaste, trim with a sharp knife and polish the surface with the curved-edge smoother. Transfer the cake on top of the board. Use the straight-edge smoother to work the paste from the base of the cake to bond into the paste on the board. Allow to dry.

**3** Position the dummy cake on top of the tilted stand and insert corsage pins through the holes in the stand and through into the polystyrene cake to hold it in place. Attach a fine band of aqua coloured ribbon around the base of both cakes using either royal icing or a small amount of softened sugarpaste to secure it in place. Attach a band of broader ribbon to the board edge using the non-toxic glue stick.

**4** Cut two lengths of the aqua beaded wire. Turn over the ends of the wire using fine-nose pliers to prevent the beads sliding off. Bend and curve the wires to create a wavy effect. Curl the ends of each. Attach the wired purple and red hearts at intervals down the length of each wire – tighten the heart wires using pliers. Attach to the underside of the dummy cake using corsage pins to hold the wire in place if required. Curl and connect the ends at the point of the heart-shaped dummy. Place the straight-edge Perspex smoother underneath the larger cake to help lift and tilt it to create a more compact overall design.

**5** Wire together the two floral sprays adding curls of aqua wire and the odd purple and red heart. Push the spray for the dummy cake directly through the sugarpaste into the polystyrene. The spray for the bottom tier needs to be pushed into a posy pick and then into the base of the cake.

| Materials | Equipment |
|---|---|
| 1.4 kg (3 lb) white sugarpaste | Sugarpaste smoothers (one curved-edge and |
| Bluegrass paste food colour (SK) | one straight-edged) |
| 15 cm (6 in) heart-shaped dummy cake | Pastry brush |
| Icing sugar | 35 cm (14 in) heart-shaped cake board |
| Clear alcohol (Cointreau or kirsch) | Sharp knife |
| Greaseproof paper | Tall Perspex tilting stand (Celcakes) |
| 25 cm (10 in) heart-shaped rich fruitcake | Large corsage pins |
| Apricot glaze | Fine-nose pliers |
| 1.25 kg (2 lb 10 oz) white almond paste | 1 posy pick (Wilton) |
| Fine aqua ribbon, to trim the cakes | |
| Broad picot-edge aqua ribbon, to trim the board | **Flowers and foliage** |
| Non-toxic glue stick (Pritt) | 2 rich red roses (see pages 40–3) |
| Aqua beaded wire | 3 dissotis flowers, plus foliage (see pages 22–3) |
| Purple and red wired hearts | 5 rothmania flowers, plus foliage (see pages 24–5) |
| 20- and 22-gauge wires | 4 spathoglottis orchids (see pages 52–3) |
| | 4 rose-hips (see pages 18–9) |
| | Assorted rosette succulents (see page 16) |

# Mother's Day

*At the time of writing this book it will be just over 20 years since I created my first floral sugarpaste cake – it was a Mother's Day cake! The cake was a green basket of multicoloured roses and silver paper leaves. Despite being a little rough round the edges my Mum loved it! Here I am using fewer flowers to great effect and I have added multicoloured auricula flowers as a reminder of my first cake.*

### Materials
*450 g (1 lb) white sugarpaste*
*Poppy paste food colour*
*15 cm (6 in) round rich fruitcake*
*Apricot glaze*
*350 g (12 oz) white almond paste*
*Icing sugar*
*Clear alcohol (Kirsch or Cointreau)*
*Fine dusky pink ribbon*
*Non-toxic craft glue stick*
*Broad aubergine braiding*
*Nile green floristry tape*
*Aubergine coloured paper-covered wire*

### Equipment
*Pastry brush*
*Rolling pin*
*Straight-edge sugarpaste smoother*
*Curved-edge sugarpaste smoother*
*23 cm (9 in) round cake board*
*Fine-nose pliers*
*Wire cutters*
*Posy pick*

### Flowers
*1 full rose (see pages 40–3)*
*9 auricula flowers, plus 7 buds (see pages 38–9)*
*15 auricula leaves (see pages 38–9)*
*3 fiddle-head ferns (see page 44)*

## PREPARATION

**1** Colour the sugarpaste with a little poppy paste food colour to create a pale flesh colour and then wrap in a plastic bag and set to one side the cake with warmed apricot glaze. Roll out the almond paste onto a fine dusting of icing sugar. Cover the cake with the paste, trimming away the excess from the base with the side of a straight-edge sugarpaste smoother. Polish the surface using the curved-edge smoother on the top of the cake and the straight-edge smoother on the sides. Allow to dry overnight.

**2** Roll out some flesh coloured sugarpaste onto a fine dusting of icing sugar. Moisten the surface of the cake with clear alcohol and cover with the sugarpaste. Trim and polish the cake as for the almond paste layer. Create a smooth finish by polishing with a pad of sugarpaste pressed into your palm.

**3** My first cake was displayed on a biscuit tin lid! It was not long before I decided I much preferred to cover the cake board with icing too! Cover the board with flesh coloured paste and transfer the cake to sit on top. Smooth the join between the base of the cake and the board using the straight-edge smoother. Allow to dry.

**4** Attach a fine band of dusky pink ribbon around the base of the cake using a tiny amount of sugarpaste softened with clear alcohol. Use the non-toxic craft glue stick to adhere the aubergine braiding to the board edge.

## FLOWERS

**5** Use the large rose as the starting point for this almost posy-style spray. Bend each of the auricula flower and leaf stems at 90-degree angles using fine-nose pliers, then tape them around the rose with half-width nile green floristry tape. Try not to position the flowers too evenly around the rose.

**6** Add the fiddle-head ferns towards the back of the rose. Finally, twist and curl some aubergine coloured paper-covered wire and tape into the spray to create a more elongated shape. Insert the handle of the spray into a posy pick and then push it into the cake.

# $\mathcal{F}$light of fancy

*Golden michelia flowers form the focal feature of this unusual, slightly Indian-themed wedding cake. The edges of the sprays are softened by adding flirting stems of dancing ladies ginger and clashing coloured butterflies, helping to create a very warm, exotic feel.*

## PREPARATION

**1** Brush both cakes with warmed apricot glaze. Roll out the almond paste on a fine dusting of icing sugar and cover with white almond paste. Allow to dry. Moisten the surface of the almond paste with clear alcohol and cover with pale yellow sugarpaste. Cover both cake boards with more of the same colour sugarpaste. Transfer the cakes to sit centrally on top of the boards. Use a straight-edge sugarpaste smoother to help blend the paste between the cake and the board.

**2** Attach a band of pink ribbon to the base of the cake using a tiny amount of sugarpaste softened with clear alcohol. Glue a band of lime ribbon to each cake board using the non-toxic glue stick. Allow the cakes to dry overnight.

**3** Tape together two floral sprays using nile green floristry tape and follow the instructions on pages 88–9. Insert the sprays into posy picks and then into the cakes. Place the small cake on top of the candleholder. Tilt the larger cake at the base by placing a Perspex smoother underneath. Add the three butterflies (see page 140), carefully pushing them into the floral sprays and resting one against the base board.

| Materials | Equipment |
|---|---|
| 10 cm (4 in) and 18 cm (7 in) rich round fruitcakes | Pastry brush |
| Apricot glaze | 15 cm (6 in) and 25 cm (10 in) round cake boards |
| 1 kg (2 lb 3 oz) white almond paste | Straight-edge sugarpaste smoother |
| Icing sugar | Ornamental candleholder |
| Clear alcohol (Cointreau or kirsch) | Perspex smoother |
| 1.4 kg (3 lb 1 oz) pale yellow sugarpaste | |
| Fine pink ribbon, to trim the cake | |
| Broad lime ribbon, to trim the board | **Flowers** |
| Non-toxic glue stick (Pritt) | 3 michelia flowers (see pages 60–2) |
| Nile green floristry tape | 18 michelia leaves (see page 62) |
| 2 posy picks | 5 stems of dancing ladies ginger (see page 30) |
| | 9 stems of string of pearls (see page 17) |
| | 6 spathoglottis orchids (see pages 52–3) |
| | 3 green butterflies (see page 140) |

# Fleurs-de-Lys

*The iris and the rose form the main focal point of this unusual*

*curved heart cake design. The blue tweedia flowers help*

*to balance the intense blue of the iris.*

### Materials

*23 cm (9 in) curved heart-shaped cake*

*Apricot glaze*

*1 kg (2 lb 3 oz) almond paste*

*Icing sugar*

*Clear alcohol (Cointreau or kirsch)*

*1.5 kg (3 lb 5 oz) white sugarpaste*

*Fine hyacinth blue ribbon*

*Non-toxic craft glue stick (Pritt)*

*Broad green velvet ribbon*

### Equipment

*Pastry brush*

*Round-edge sugarpaste smoother*

*Straight-edge sugarpaste smoother*

*33 cm (13 in) curved heart-shaped cake board*

*Wire cutters*

*Nile green floristry tape*

*Posy pick*

*18-gauge wire wires*

### Flowers

*1 full rose, plus 3 sets of leaves (see pages 40–3)*

*1 iris and 1 bud (see pages 46–9)*

*3 stems of tweedia (see pages 28–9)*

*1 green gloriosa lily, plus foliage (see page 80–1)*

*5 polyalthia flowers (see page 32)*

**PREPARATION**

**1** Brush the cake with warmed apricot glaze. Roll out the almond paste on a fine dusting of icing sugar and cover the cake. Allow to dry overnight.

**2** Moisten the surface of the almond paste with clear alcohol and cover with sugarpaste. Use sugarpaste smoothers to polish and neaten the top and sides of the cake. This shape can be tricky to polish so you will find a pad of sugarpaste pushed into your palm very useful for polishing the edges and awkward curves.

**3** Cover the cake board with sugarpaste and position the cake centrally on top. Use the straight-edge smoother to blend the join between the cake and the board.

**4** Attach a band of blue ribbon around the base of the cake, using a tiny amount of sugarpaste softened with clear alcohol. Use the non-toxic craft glue stick to adhere the broad green velvet ribbon to the board edge.

**FLOWERS**

**5** I have arranged these flowers almost like a hand-tied bunch of flowers, using both the rose and the iris as the main features and adding the remaining flowers around them. Trim away excess wires as you work with wire cutters. Tape the flowers together using half-width nile green floristry tape. Push the posy pick into the side of the cake and fill it with almond paste. Position the handle of the spray against the hole and 'clip' into the pick using 'hairpin' bends of 18-gauge wire pushing the wire into the almond paste.

# $\mathcal{P}$ink paradise

*Pink pavonia and hibiscus flowers are combined with assorted foliage to create a striking floral display on this cake that would be suitable for a small wedding or perhaps even as an anniversary or birthday cake.*

## PREPARATION

**1** Brush the cake with warmed apricot glaze. Roll out the almond paste onto a light dusting of icing sugar. Cover the cake and trim away excess paste. Smooth the top of the cake with a curved sugarpaste smoother and the sides with a straight-edge smoother. Allow to dry overnight.

**2** Moisten the surface of the almond paste with clear alcohol and cover with white sugarpaste. Use the smoothers as before and then create a more polished finish with a ball of sugarpaste pressed into your palm. Cover the cake board with sugarpaste and transfer the cake to sit on top. Work the base of the cake with the straight-edge smoother to blend the cake and the board together. Allow to dry overnight.

**3** Attach a band of fine pink ribbon to the base of the cake using sugarpaste softened with clear alcohol. Glue a band of lime green ribbon to the board edge using the non-toxic craft glue stick.

## FLOWERS

**4** Use the hibiscus flower as the focal point of the spray. Add the pavonia flowers evenly spaced around the hibiscus, taping them onto the main stem with half-width nile green floristry tape. Bend each stem to a 90-degree angle as you add them to the spray.

**5** Next, add the hibiscus foliage and buds followed by the trails of string of pearl succulents. Insert the handle of the spray into a posy pick and then push it directly into the cake. Re-arrange the flowers slightly to create a more relaxed overall finish.

### Materials

20 cm (8 in) oval rich fruitcake

Apricot glaze

750 g (1 lb 10 oz) white almond paste

Icing sugar

Clear alcohol (Cointreau or kirsch)

1 kg (2 lb 3 oz) white sugarpaste

Fine pink ribbon, to trim the cake

Broad lime green ribbon, to trim the board

Non-toxic craft glue stick (Pritt)

Nile green floristry tape

Posy pick

### Equipment

Pastry brush

Rolling pin

Curved sugarpaste smoother

Straight-edge sugarpaste smoother

30 cm (12 in) oval cake board

Fine-nose pliers

Wire cutters

### Flowers

1 hibiscus flower (see pages 78–9)

3 pavonia flowers (see pages 50–1)

9 hibiscus leaves (see page 79)

2 hibiscus buds (see page 79)

7 trails of string of pearls (see page 17)

# Snake vine cake

*I could not resist using snakeskin-effect ribbon on this cake. I spent a small fortune buying ribbons for this book – sadly, department stores are selling reduced ranges which often means it is harder to find interesting ribbon at reasonable prices. I am not a huge fan of the colour yellow so when I do use it I add darker colours to calm it down slightly!*

### Materials

*20 cm (8 in) heart-shaped rich fruitcake*
*Apricot glaze*
*750 g (1 lb 10 oz) white almond paste*
*Icing sugar*
*Clear alcohol (Cointreau or kirsch)*
*1 kg (2 lb 3 oz) white sugarpaste*
*Green and cream decorative braid*
*Snakeskin-effect ribbon*
*Non-toxic craft glue stick (Pritt)*
*Small amount of flowerpaste*
*Edible gold leaf (SK)*
*Vine green and foliage petal dusts*
*Nile green floristry tape*
*Gold, brown and beige paper-covered wire*
*Posy pick*

### Equipment

*Pastry brush*
*Round-edge sugarpaste smoother*
*Straight-edge sugarpaste smoother*
*30 cm (12 in) heart-shaped board*
*Couple of pins*
*Large, soft brush*
*Scroll and comma cutters (LS)*
*Fine paintbrush*

### Flowers

*3 snake vine flowers (see pages 64–5)*
*30 snake vine leaves (see page 66)*
*3 snake vine buds (see page 66)*

## PREPARATION

1 Brush the cake with warmed apricot glaze. Roll out the almond paste on a fine dusting of icing sugar, then polish the surface with a round-edge sugarpaste smoother and cover the cake with the almond paste. Trim away the excess paste from around the base of the cake using the straight-edge smoother. Polish the surface again using the round-edge smoother on the top of the cake and the straight-edge smoother on the sides. Allow to dry overnight.

2 Moisten the surface of the almond paste with clear alcohol. Roll out the white sugarpaste onto a fine dusting of icing sugar and cover the cake. Use the smoothers as above and then use a pad of sugarpaste pressed into your palm to smooth and polish the surface of the cake further. Cover the board with sugarpaste and transfer the cake on top. Use the straight-edge smoother to blend the join between the cake and the board. Allow to dry overnight.

3 Attach a band of green and cream braid to the base of the cake using a tiny amount of sugarpaste softened with clear alcohol. Fold the snakeskin-effect ribbon to make it fit the depth of the cake board and attach using the non-toxic glue stick and a couple of pins pushed into the back of the board to hold it in place.

## GOLD LEAF DESIGN

4 Roll out some well-kneaded flowerpaste onto a non-stick board. Turn the paste over so that it is 'sticky'-side up. Carefully remove a sheet of gold leaf and place it onto the flowerpaste. Remove the backing paper. Brush gently over the surface with a large, soft brush to bond the two mediums.

5 Cut out some decorative curved shapes using the scroll- and comma-shaped cutters. Attach to the surface of the cake and the baseboard using a little clear alcohol. Mix together vine green and foliage petal dusts and dilute with a little clear alcohol. Paint a series of small dots around the gold leaf design to create a slightly softer design finish.

## FLOWERS

6 Tape together two snake vine flowers using half-width nile green floristry tape. Add trails of snake vine leaves and buds to create a long reversed 'S' shaped spray. Plait together some gold, brown and beige paper-covered wire – not too neatly. Tangle the plait in amongst the flowers and allow it to 'snake' its way through the spray, curling it at the very tip. Insert the spray into a posy pick and then into the cake. Wire a smaller spray with a single snake vine flower and trails of foliage and plaited wires. Rest the small spray against the cake board.

# Elegance

*Despite being large in form, magnolias have a very peaceful, elegant aura. They work well with other flowers but I feel they are at there best used in a simple arrangement. The floral pearl design on the surface of the cake was created using large magnolia patchwork cutters.*

## PREPARATION

**1** Brush the cake with warmed apricot glaze and cover with white almond paste. Allow to dry. Place the cake onto a sheet of greaseproof paper. Moisten the surface with clear alcohol and cover with the sugarpaste. Trim away the excess from the base of the cake and smooth over the surface with sugarpaste smoothers and also a pad of sugarpaste pressed into the palm to polish the surface of the cake and neaten the tight curl of the teardrop shape.

## EMBOSSED DESIGN

**2** Quickly create the embossed floral design by pressing two sizes of magnolia patchwork cutters into the surface of the paste. Allow to dry.

**3** Remove the cake from the greaseproof paper and transfer onto the Perspex board. Attach a band of velvet ribbon around the base of the cake using a small amount of royal icing or sugarpaste softened with clear alcohol to secure it.

**4** Melt a small amount of cocoa butter on a saucer above a mug of just boiled water. Add edelweiss petal dust and a touch of plum to form a paint to colour in the large petal area of the embossed design. Gradually add more plum to add veins and depth to each of the petals using a slightly finer brush. Treat the leaves in the same way, starting with a pale bright vine green base gradually building in layers with foliage and aubergine edges. Paint in the main stems using aubergine and foliage mixed together. Add curled dotted lines to soften the edges of the design using a mixture of vine green and foliage petal dusts. Allow to dry, then dust the surface with bridal satin to give a pearl effect.

**5** Attach a ball of white florists' stay soft onto the Perspex board at the base of the cake and arrange the stems of magnolia flowers and foliage into it to curve around the cake. Use extra leaves to hide and disguise any excess stay soft that may be visible.

### Materials

*20-cm (8-in) teardrop-shaped rich fruitcake*

*Apricot glaze*

*750 g (1 lb 10 oz) white almond paste*

*Greaseproof paper*

*Clear alcohol (Cointreau or kirsch)*

*750 g (1 lb 10 oz) white sugarpaste*

*Soft grey-green velvet ribbon, to trim the cake*

*Cocoa butter*

*Mug and saucer*

*Edelweiss, plum, vine green, foliage, aubergine and bridal satin petal dusts*

*Assorted paintbrushes*

### Equipment

*Sugarpaste smoothers*

*Magnolia patchwork cutters (PWC)*

*35-cm (14-in) oval Perspex cake board*

*White florists' stay soft*

### Flowers

*2 magnolia flowers (see page 63)*

*2 magnolia buds (see page 63)*

*7 magnolia leaves (see page 63)*

# Sugar butterflies

*The sugar butterflies on this cake were made by my Australian friend John Quoi Hoi. They were posted from Australia for use on a cake that my friend Tombi and I were creating for an exhibition a while ago. It is amazing that the butterflies survived the flight from Australia to the UK!*

### Materials

*White flowerpaste*
*26- and 28-gauge white wires*
*Scissors*
*Black food paste colour*
*Egg white*
*Sharp scalpel*
*Black stamens*
*Spring, moss, foliage, primrose and egg yellow petal dusts*
*Nile green floristry tape*

### Equipment

*Butterfly cutters (J)*
*Black non-toxic craft pen*
*Dusting brush*

## WINGS

**1** The wings of this butterfly are all individually wired with 28-gauge wire, as is the body. The colouring is that of a bird wing butterfly and some artistic licence has been taken. Roll out some white flowerpaste relatively thinly with a thicker ridge down the middle.

**2** Cut out the wing shape using the wing cutter, making sure the ridge is in the middle and about two thirds the length of the cutter. Cut a piece of 28-gauge white wire, moisten and then thread it into the ridge. Flatten the flowerpaste onto the wire and neaten the base. Allow to dry flat. Make two wing shapes.

**3** Follow the same procedure with the base wing, using the smaller cutter. Make sure each is a mirror image of the other. Allow to dry thoroughly before colouring. Make two base wings.

## BODY

**4** The body is made by mixing some flowerpaste with a little black food paste colour. Roll a pea-size amount of flowerpaste into a carrot shape. Take a 26-gauge white wire and form a small closed hook at one end. Bend to a small figure 7. Dip this end into a little egg white and thread into the middle part of the body. Neaten the base.

**5** Mark the body with a sharp scalpel to form the butterfly's head, and upper and lower body. Cut a black stamen in half. Insert into the head of the body and allow to dry. When dry, you can curl back the stamens to give some movement. Colouring the flower paste black first saves you painting the body later.

## COLOURING

**6** I use a non-toxic black pen to draw the lines and colour in the black on the wings. Paint the edges of the wings with black as well. Do this first before dusting.

**7** To colour the wings, dust from the outside edge in with spring green petal dust both on the front and back of all four wings. Then over-dust lightly with some moss green or foliage green. Finally, dust from the wired end with some primrose and egg yellow petal dusts.

## ASSEMBLY

**8** Using half-width nile green floristry tape, tape the top wings to the body, then the bottom wings. Adjust the wings, then steam the butterfly to set the dusts.

# Templates

These templates are supplied at 100 per cent and should be photocopied or traced at the sizes shown.

Page 28
**TWEEDIA LEAVES**

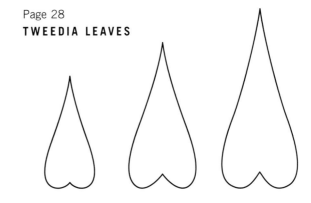

Page 45
**CROTON LEAVES**

Page 56
**DILLENIA PETAL**

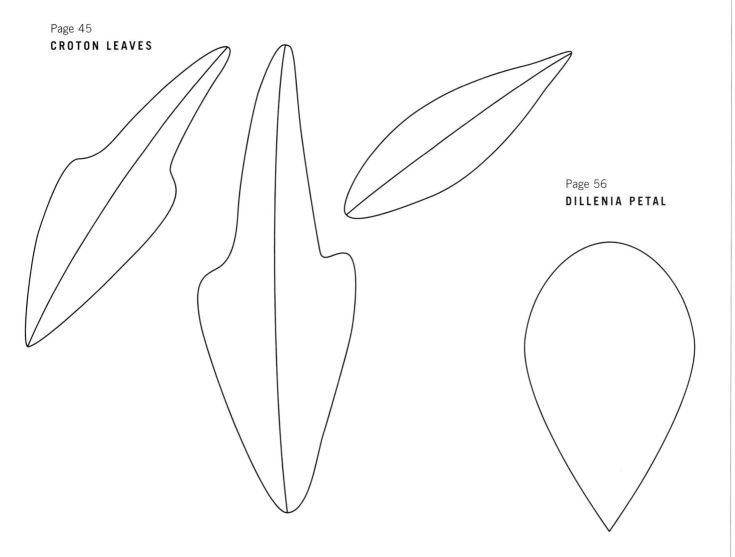

Page 80
## GLORIOSA LILY PETAL AND LEAF

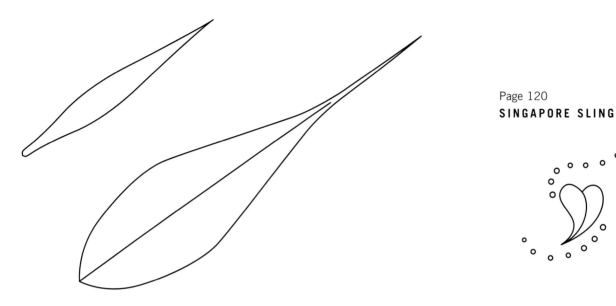

Page 120
## SINGAPORE SLING

Page 112
## SIAMESE CA

Page 124
**ORCHID TRAIL SIDE DESIGN**

Page 126
**EVERLASTING
LOVE CAKE**

Page 140
**BUTTERFLY WINGS**

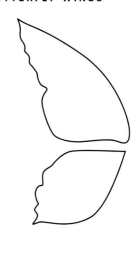

**Alan Dunn**
Nasturtium72@aol.com

**A Piece of Cake** (flowerpaste,
Fabilo spray varnish, fine cotton
thread and lots more)
18 Upper High Street
Thame
Oxon OX9 3EX
sales@sugaricing.com

**Aldaval Veiners (ALDV)** (petal/leaf
veiners and dummy cakes)
16 Chibburn Court
Widdrington
Morpeth
Northumberland NE61 5QT
+44 (0)1670 790995

**Cakes, Classes and Cutters**
23 Princes Road
Brunton Park
Gosforth
Newcastle-upon-Tyne NE3 5TT
+44 (0)191 2170538

**Celcakes and Celcrafts (Cc)**
Springfield House
Gate Helmsley
York YO4 1NF
www.celcrafts.co.uk

**Confectionery Supplies**
31 Lower Cathedral Road
Cardiff
Gwent NP5 4BQ
+44 (0)1600 740448

**Culpitt Cake Art**
Jubilee Industrial Estate
Ashington
Northumberland NE63 8UQ
+44 (0)1670 814545

**Design-a-Cake**
30–31 Phoenix Road,
Crowther Industrial Estate
Washington
Tyne & Wear NE38 0AD
enquiry@design-a-cake.co.uk

**Guy, Paul & Co. Ltd** (UK distributor
for Jem cutters)
Unit 10
The Business Centre
Corinium Industrial Estate
Raans Road
Amersham
Bucks HP6 6EB
sales@guypaul.co.uk

**ECG Supplies**
844 North Crowley Road
Crowley
TX 76036
USA
www.europeancakegallery.us

**Holly products (HP)**
Primrose Cottage
Church Walk
Norton in Hales
Shropshire TF9 4QX
enquiries@hollyproducts.co.uk

**Lindy Smith (LS)**
17 Grenville Avenue
Wendover
Aylesbury
Buckinghamshire HP22 6AG
+44 (0)1296 623906

**Orchard Products (OPR)**
51 Hallyburton Road
Hove
East Sussex BN3 7GP
+44 (0)1273 419418

**The British Sugarcraft Guild**
(a wonderful starting point for any
sugarcrafter. For more information
about your nearest branch contact:
www.bsg.org

**The Old Bakery** (Japanese stamens
and wires)
Kingston St Mary
Taunton
Sommerset TA2 8HW
+44 (0)1823 451205

**The Secret Garden** (Florist)
19 Clayton Road
Jesmond
Newcastle upon Tyne
+44 (0)191 281 7753

**Jem Cutters (J)**
PO Box 115
Kloof 3640
South Africa
0027 31 701 1431

**Patchwork Cutters (PWC)**
123 Saughall Massie Road
Upton
Wirral CH49 4LA
www.patchworkcutters.com

**Renshaw** (regalice sugarpaste)
Crown Street
Liverpool L8 7RF
+44 (0)870 870 6954

**Tinkertech Two (TT)**
40 Langdon Road
Parkstone
Poole
Dorset BH14 9EH
+44 (0)1202 738049

**Squires Kitchen (SKGI)** (edible gold
leaf, cocoa butter, petal/leaf
veiners and petal dusts)
Squires House
3 Waverley Lane
Farnham
Surrey GU9 8BB
www.squires-shop.com

**V V Rouleaux** (ribbons)
38 Brentwood Avenue
Jesmond
Newcastle upon Tyne NE2 3DH
newcastle@vvrouleaux.com

**Wilton (W)**
Knightsbridge Bakeware Centre Ltd
Chadwell Heath Lane
Romford
Essex RM6 4NP

# *J*ndex